Building Smart Homes with Raspberry Pi and IoT Sensor

Create intelligent home automation systems using open-source technology

THOMPSON CARTER

Table of Content

TABLE OF CONTENTS

Introduction

Building Smart Homes with Raspberry Pi and IoT Sensors

In today's world, home automation has evolved from a futuristic concept to a practical reality that is reshaping how we interact with our living spaces. A smart home isn't just about convenience; it's about creating a living environment that is more efficient, secure, comfortable, and tailored to the unique needs of its inhabitants. With the rapid rise of the **Internet of Things (IoT)** and the affordability and flexibility of **Raspberry Pi**, building a smart home is no longer reserved for the tech-savvy elite. It's a project that anyone can take on, regardless of experience, to create a fully automated, connected home.

This book is designed to guide you through the entire journey of building your own smart home, from the foundational concepts to the advanced integration of devices and systems. With the power of **Raspberry Pi** and **IoT sensors**, you'll be able to bring various devices to life, automate your home environment, and enhance your daily living experience with minimal complexity. Whether you are

11

looking to start small with a few smart devices or embark on a comprehensive automation project, this book provides a step-by-step, easy-to-follow approach to transforming your home into a truly smart space.

Why Raspberry Pi?

At the heart of the DIY smart home revolution lies the **Raspberry Pi**, a compact, affordable, and powerful single-board computer that serves as the perfect tool for building a smart home hub. Whether you're a hobbyist looking to experiment with automation or someone seeking a practical and cost-effective way to upgrade your home, **Raspberry Pi** is a versatile platform that provides endless possibilities. It allows you to create a centralized hub to control various IoT devices, making it easier to integrate a wide variety of sensors, cameras, thermostats, lights, and more.

Through this book, you'll learn how to leverage **Raspberry Pi**'s capabilities, turning it into the brain of your home automation system. From setting up your Pi to communicating with IoT devices, you'll discover how to build robust systems that go beyond simple automation to provide powerful intelligence and interactivity.

Exploring IoT Sensors

One of the driving forces behind smart homes is **IoT sensors**. These sensors provide critical data about the environment, allowing devices to interact with their surroundings and make intelligent decisions. Sensors can monitor temperature, humidity, motion, light levels, and even air quality, creating the foundation for responsive, dynamic environments.

This book introduces a wide range of sensors—motion detectors, temperature and humidity sensors, smart lights, and security cameras—that you can integrate with your **Raspberry Pi** to enhance your home's functionality. You'll learn how to wire these sensors, configure them to communicate with your Raspberry Pi, and use them for specific automation tasks. Whether it's adjusting your thermostat based on the room's temperature or triggering an alarm when motion is detected, IoT sensors enable your home to adapt to your lifestyle automatically.

Creating Personalized Automation Systems

One of the most rewarding aspects of building a smart home is the ability to personalize the system to meet your unique

13

needs. Automation is at the heart of this personalization. With this book, you'll learn how to create intelligent automation systems that can handle tasks ranging from simple (like turning off the lights when you leave a room) to complex (such as scheduling the coffee maker to brew at a specific time every morning or adjusting the home's lighting and temperature based on the time of day).

Automation not only saves you time and energy, but it also contributes to a more sustainable, comfortable home. You'll be able to set up routines and triggers that are completely customized to your preferences, from energy-saving settings to personalized ambiance adjustments.

Advanced Features: Integrating AI, Machine Learning, and Security

As your smart home grows, so does the complexity and potential for advanced features. This book also delves into the integration of **AI** and **machine learning** to create predictive, adaptive systems that can learn from your behavior and make intelligent decisions about your home. Imagine a system that adjusts your heating and lighting based on your activity patterns or detects security threats by learning typical activity around the house.

In addition to automation, the book covers key aspects of **security**, an essential component of any smart home. You'll learn how to implement effective security systems, from **smart locks** and **cameras** to **motion detectors** that help safeguard your home. These devices can be monitored and controlled remotely, giving you peace of mind whether you're at home or away.

Expanding and Scaling Your Smart Home

A smart home is not a static project; it's one that grows with you. As you become more familiar with the technologies, you'll want to expand your system. This book explores how to scale your smart home, adding more devices and sensors while ensuring everything works harmoniously. You'll also learn how to manage multiple **Raspberry Pi** devices, expand your network, and integrate third-party devices into your system seamlessly.

Whether you're scaling your system from a small setup to a larger one or integrating new IoT devices from different manufacturers, this book helps you build a flexible, adaptable smart home that meets your evolving needs.

Real-World Applications and Examples

This book is not just about theory—it's about practical, hands-on projects that can be implemented in real-world environments. Throughout the chapters, you'll find detailed examples and step-by-step instructions for building smart home systems that can be implemented right away. Each chapter includes clear, actionable guidance to help you design, build, and deploy your own smart home systems using **Raspberry Pi** and **IoT sensors**.

Conclusion

Building a smart home with **Raspberry Pi** and **IoT sensors** is an exciting and empowering experience that allows you to take full control over your living environment. Whether you are a beginner or someone with a bit of experience in tech, this book will equip you with the knowledge and skills to turn your home into a smart, automated, and efficient space.

By the end of this book, you'll not only have created a personalized smart home but also gained valuable insights into home automation that you can continue to explore and expand on. The journey to creating your own smart home has never been more accessible, and this book is your guide to making it a reality.

Let's begin the journey of building a smarter, more connected home—one that learns from you, adapts to your needs, and offers a higher level of convenience, security, and sustainability than ever before.

CHAPTER 1

INTRODUCTION TO SMART HOMES AND HOME AUTOMATION

Smart homes are the future of living, where technology enhances the comfort, convenience, security, and energy efficiency of everyday life. At their core, smart homes use internet-connected devices that can be remotely controlled or automated to make a home smarter. These devices, often referred to as "smart devices," include lights, thermostats, locks, security cameras, and appliances, all designed to communicate with each other and with the homeowner's phone or voice assistant.

How Home Automation Works

Home automation is the process of using technology to control various functions of a home automatically. Rather than manually adjusting the thermostat or switching off lights, home automation systems can make these changes on their own based on triggers or schedules. For instance, your lights might turn on automatically when you enter a room, or the heating system might kick on when the temperature drops below a certain point. These systems can often be controlled remotely, providing ultimate convenience for users.

The key technologies that make home automation possible are sensors, actuators, and smart hubs. Sensors detect changes in the environment (e.g., motion, temperature, or light levels), and actuators perform tasks like turning on lights or adjusting the thermostat. Smart hubs act as the central control point, allowing all devices to communicate with each other, either via a smartphone app or voice commands.

Key Benefits and Challenges of Building a Smart Home

Building a smart home comes with its own set of advantages and challenges.

Benefits:

1. **Convenience**: Smart homes make everyday tasks much easier. You can control your home's lighting, temperature, and security systems from anywhere in the world, using just your smartphone.

2. **Energy Efficiency**: Automating your home can reduce energy consumption by optimizing the use of heating, cooling, and lighting. Smart thermostats can adjust the temperature based on your behavior, while smart lights turn off when not needed.

3. **Security**: Smart security systems, such as cameras, motion detectors, and smart locks, provide real-time alerts and allow you to monitor your home remotely. Many systems can even integrate with emergency services for immediate responses.

4. **Comfort**: With sensors that monitor temperature and humidity, your home can automatically adjust to create the perfect living environment, making it more comfortable year-round.

Challenges:

1. **Cost**: Setting up a fully automated smart home can be expensive. The cost of smart devices, installation, and software can add up, especially if you're outfitting an entire house.

2. **Complexity**: While the idea of a smart home is exciting, the technical complexity can be overwhelming, especially for beginners. Integrating different devices and ensuring they work together smoothly can require some technical know-how.

3. **Privacy and Security**: With so many devices connected to the internet, security risks such as hacking or data breaches are a concern. It's crucial to ensure that each device is properly secured and that data is protected.

4. **Compatibility**: Not all smart devices are compatible with each other, particularly if you are using devices from different manufacturers. Choosing a platform or hub that supports multiple device types can help mitigate this issue.

The Role of Raspberry Pi and IoT in Transforming Ordinary Homes into Smart Ones

Raspberry Pi, a small and affordable computer, plays a vital role in transforming traditional homes into smart homes. It acts as the backbone for many DIY smart home projects, providing a flexible and customizable platform for controlling IoT (Internet of Things) devices. By integrating sensors, relays, and actuators with Raspberry Pi, users can create their own home automation systems, which can be customized to meet their specific needs.

IoT sensors are at the heart of smart homes, allowing devices to communicate with one another and with users. These sensors gather data from the home environment (such as temperature, humidity, and motion) and send it to Raspberry

Pi for analysis. Raspberry Pi can then make decisions or trigger actions based on this data, such as turning on a fan when the room becomes too hot or sending a notification if the security system detects movement.

Together, Raspberry Pi and IoT sensors allow homeowners to build affordable, highly customizable smart home systems that can be controlled and automated in real-time, often without the need for expensive proprietary systems. They also offer a way to keep up with technological advancements while using open-source tools, providing endless possibilities for innovation and expansion.

CHAPTER 2

UNDERSTANDING THE RASPBERRY PI

The Raspberry Pi is a small, affordable computer that has taken the tech world by storm, particularly for projects involving IoT (Internet of Things) and home automation. In this chapter, we'll dive into the hardware, various models, and how Raspberry Pi fits seamlessly into the smart home ecosystem. We'll also guide you through the steps of setting up your Raspberry Pi for the first time, making it ready for all your home automation projects.

Detailed Explanation of Raspberry Pi Hardware, Models, and Capabilities

Raspberry Pi is often described as a single-board computer because all the core components — the processor, memory, and input/output pins — are all integrated into one compact board. Despite its small size, the Raspberry Pi packs significant computing power, making it perfect for a wide range of DIY projects, from basic education to sophisticated smart home automation systems.

Here's a breakdown of key components typically found in Raspberry Pi boards:

- **Processor (CPU)**: Raspberry Pi uses ARM-based processors, which are efficient and capable of running a wide range of software. The newer models come with faster processors for improved performance.
- **Memory (RAM)**: Depending on the model, Raspberry Pi offers different amounts of RAM, typically ranging from 1GB to 8GB. More RAM allows for more intensive tasks, such as running a web server or processing large sensor data sets.
- **Storage**: Instead of having a built-in hard drive, Raspberry Pi relies on an SD card for storage. The SD card holds the operating system and data, so it's essential to choose a high-quality card with adequate space.
- **Ports**: Raspberry Pi models come with various USB ports, HDMI outputs for connecting to displays, and GPIO (General Purpose Input/Output) pins for connecting sensors, motors, and other electronics.
- **Networking**: Most models include Ethernet ports for wired connections and Wi-Fi for wireless connectivity, making it easy to connect to your home network.

Raspberry Pi Models

Several versions of the Raspberry Pi are available, each with varying capabilities, making it important to select the right one based on your needs.

- **Raspberry Pi 4 Model B**: This is the most powerful model in the Raspberry Pi lineup, offering multiple RAM options (2GB, 4GB, or 8GB) and improved processing power. It's great for tasks that require significant performance, like handling multiple IoT sensors or streaming data.
- **Raspberry Pi 3 Model B+**: The Raspberry Pi 3 is slightly older but still highly capable. It includes built-in Wi-Fi and Bluetooth support and is well-suited for general IoT projects and home automation tasks.
- **Raspberry Pi Zero W**: If you need a smaller, less expensive option for basic projects, the Raspberry Pi Zero W is perfect. It's a more compact version with fewer ports but still includes Wi-Fi and Bluetooth for wireless communication.

How Raspberry Pi Fits into the Smart Home Ecosystem

Raspberry Pi plays a central role in transforming traditional homes into smart homes. It acts as the "brain" of many home automation systems, connecting various IoT sensors and devices to a central hub that can be controlled via a smartphone, tablet, or voice assistant.

Some key applications of Raspberry Pi in smart homes include:

- **Control Hub**: Raspberry Pi can act as a central hub that communicates with and controls all your smart home devices. With tools like Home Assistant or OpenHAB, you can use Raspberry Pi to create a seamless integration system for managing lights, thermostats, security cameras, and more.

- **Sensor Management**: Raspberry Pi is perfect for handling data from various sensors, like temperature, humidity, and motion sensors. It can process this data, trigger actions (such as turning on the lights or adjusting the thermostat), and send alerts to your phone.

- **Automation Engine**: Raspberry Pi can run automation scripts and programs to make your home smarter. For instance, you can create rules like "When motion is detected in the living room, turn on the lights." With Raspberry Pi, these automation systems can be as simple or complex as you need.

- **Voice Assistants**: Raspberry Pi can be used to set up your own voice-controlled assistant, like Amazon Alexa or Google Assistant, by using software libraries that allow you to control your home with simple voice commands.

Setting Up Your Raspberry Pi for the First Time (Operating Systems, Initial Configurations)

Getting your Raspberry Pi up and running for the first time is straightforward. Here's a step-by-step guide to setting it up:

1. **Install the Operating System (OS)**
   - Raspberry Pi does not come with an operating system pre-installed, so you'll need to install one yourself. The official OS is **Raspberry Pi OS** (previously known as Raspbian), which is a Debian-based operating system.
   - To install the OS, download the **Raspberry Pi Imager** from the official Raspberry Pi website. This software allows you to flash the operating system onto an SD card.
   - Insert the SD card into your computer, select **Raspberry Pi OS** in the Imager, and write it to the card.

2. **Insert the SD Card and Boot the Raspberry Pi**
   - Once the OS is installed, insert the SD card into the Raspberry Pi. Connect a monitor, keyboard, and mouse to the Pi.
   - Power up the Raspberry Pi by plugging it into a power source. The Pi will boot from the SD card

and guide you through the initial setup process, including choosing your language, Wi-Fi network, and setting up the password.

3. **Update and Upgrade Your System**

   o   After the first boot, it's important to update the system to ensure you have the latest software and security patches.

   o   Open a terminal window and run the following commands:

```
sql
```

```
sudo apt update
sudo apt upgrade
```

   o   This ensures that all the latest updates are installed.

4. **Enable SSH and VNC for Remote Access**

   o   For convenience, you can enable **SSH** (Secure Shell) to remotely access your Raspberry Pi from another computer or mobile device. This allows you to control the Pi without needing a monitor and keyboard connected.

   o   To enable SSH, open the **Raspberry Pi Configuration** tool and navigate to the **Interfaces** tab. Enable SSH and reboot the Pi.

- o   You can also enable **VNC** (Virtual Network Computing) for graphical remote access to your Pi's desktop.

5. **Connect to the Internet**

- o   If you haven't already connected to Wi-Fi during the setup, you can do so later by clicking the Wi-Fi icon in the top-right corner of the screen and selecting your network.
- o   For Ethernet connections, simply plug the Ethernet cable into the Raspberry Pi.

6. **Install Essential Software**

- o   Now that your Raspberry Pi is set up, you can install additional software packages depending on your project's needs. For home automation, tools like **Node-RED, Home Assistant**, and **OpenHAB** are popular for controlling IoT devices.
- o   You can also install Python libraries for various sensors and devices, such as **RPi.GPIO** for interacting with GPIO pins.

With these steps, your Raspberry Pi is ready to be integrated into your smart home system. Whether you're creating a simple home automation project or a complex multi-device network, the Raspberry Pi offers endless possibilities for transforming your home into an intelligent, connected space.

CHAPTER 3

GETTING STARTED WITH IOT (INTERNET OF THINGS)

The Internet of Things (IoT) has revolutionized the way we interact with the world around us, particularly in the realm of smart homes. In this chapter, we will explore the concept of IoT, how it connects devices in a smart home, and the essential IoT sensors and protocols that help make home automation possible.

Introduction to IoT and How It Connects Devices Within a Smart Home

The Internet of Things (IoT) refers to the network of physical devices that are embedded with sensors, software, and other technologies, enabling them to connect and exchange data over the internet. In a smart home, IoT devices can communicate with each other, often without direct human intervention, making everyday tasks more automated and efficient.

At the core of IoT in a smart home is the ability for devices to "talk" to each other, creating a cohesive, interconnected environment. For example, motion sensors can trigger the lights to turn on when someone enters a room, while a smart thermostat can adjust the temperature based on occupancy detected by motion sensors. Through IoT, each device sends data, receives commands, and responds according to pre-configured rules or triggers, enabling homeowners to control their environment in a seamless way.

These interactions are often controlled remotely through smartphones, voice assistants (such as Amazon Alexa or Google Assistant), or web interfaces, allowing you to monitor and adjust your home automation system from virtually anywhere.

Types of IoT Sensors Used in Smart Homes

To make a home "smart," various sensors are used to gather real-time data and enable automated responses. Here are some common IoT sensors used in smart homes:

1. **Temperature and Humidity Sensors**: These sensors monitor the temperature and humidity levels within the home. Smart thermostats use this data to

adjust the heating or cooling systems, ensuring optimal comfort while also improving energy efficiency. They are often used to regulate indoor climates based on environmental factors or set schedules.

2. **Motion Sensors (PIR Sensors)**: Passive Infrared (PIR) motion sensors detect movement within a room. These are essential for automating lights, fans, or even security systems. For instance, when motion is detected in a hallway, the lights may automatically turn on.

3. **Light Sensors**: These sensors detect the intensity of light in a room or an outdoor area. They are often used for automatic lighting control, adjusting indoor lighting based on the amount of natural sunlight entering the room.

4. **Smoke and Gas Sensors**: Safety is a top priority in smart homes, and smoke and gas sensors provide essential protection by detecting harmful gases like carbon monoxide or smoke. These sensors can trigger alarms or send alerts to your phone, ensuring that safety measures are taken promptly.

5. **Door and Window Sensors**: These sensors monitor the status of doors and windows, ensuring that they

are properly closed or alerting homeowners when a door or window is left open. They are commonly used in security systems to detect potential break-ins.

6. **Security Cameras**: While not technically a "sensor" in the traditional sense, security cameras are an integral part of the smart home ecosystem. They provide real-time video feeds and motion detection alerts, helping homeowners keep an eye on their property remotely.

7. **Sound Sensors**: These sensors detect changes in sound levels. For example, they can be used in a smart home security system to recognize specific noises, such as glass breaking, and trigger alarms or notifications.

8. **Pressure Sensors**: Pressure sensors can detect weight or pressure changes. They are used in applications such as automated pet feeders or smart beds, which monitor sleeping patterns or movement.

Overview of IoT Protocols (MQTT, HTTP, etc.)

For IoT devices to communicate effectively, they rely on specific protocols. These protocols are sets of rules that define how data is transmitted and received between devices over a network. Here are a few important IoT communication protocols that play a crucial role in smart home systems:

1. **MQTT (Message Queuing Telemetry Transport)**: MQTT is a lightweight and efficient messaging protocol that is widely used in IoT applications. It operates on a publisher-subscriber model, where devices (publishers) send data to a central server (broker), and other devices (subscribers) receive that data. MQTT is perfect for situations where devices need to communicate in real-time with low bandwidth, making it ideal for home automation. It's commonly used to send sensor data, like temperature readings, and for sending control commands, such as turning on lights or adjusting thermostats.

   Key Features:

   o Low bandwidth usage, making it ideal for low-power devices.
   o Real-time communication with minimal delay.
   o Reliable delivery, even over unstable networks.

2. **HTTP (Hypertext Transfer Protocol)**: HTTP is the most common protocol used for communication on the web. It's also used in many IoT systems for

communication between smart home devices and servers. HTTP is simple to implement, but it can be slower and less efficient compared to MQTT, especially when handling a large number of devices.

Key Features:

- o Well-established and widely supported.
- o Uses the request-response model, where a device sends a request to a server and waits for a response.
- o Best for applications where real-time communication isn't critical.

3. **CoAP (Constrained Application Protocol)**: CoAP is a protocol designed for resource-constrained devices, offering a lightweight method of communication that works well over low-bandwidth and high-latency networks. It is often used in conjunction with sensors and actuators in IoT systems.

Key Features:

- o Very low overhead, making it efficient for small devices with limited processing power.

- o Supports multicast, which is beneficial for controlling multiple devices at once.
- o Designed for use in environments where bandwidth is limited or unreliable.

4. **Zigbee**: Zigbee is a wireless communication protocol commonly used for creating mesh networks of IoT devices. It is designed for short-range communication and low-power devices, making it ideal for smart home applications such as lighting and security systems. Zigbee enables devices to communicate directly with each other, which can improve reliability and range.

Key Features:

- o Low power consumption, suitable for battery-operated devices.
- o Mesh networking, where devices can relay messages to extend coverage.
- o Secure communication with built-in encryption.

5. **Bluetooth Low Energy (BLE)**: Bluetooth Low Energy (BLE) is a wireless communication protocol that is energy-efficient and suitable for short-range communication. It's often used in smart home devices like fitness trackers, door locks, and smart speakers. BLE devices are typically used for

communication within a range of up to 100 meters, and they are known for their minimal power usage.

Key Features:

- o Low energy consumption, perfect for battery-powered devices.
- o Short-range communication, making it ideal for local smart home devices.
- o Popular in wearable devices and personal electronics.

Conclusion

IoT is the backbone of the modern smart home, enabling devices to communicate and collaborate to automate tasks and enhance living spaces. Sensors provide the data needed to monitor and control the environment, while IoT protocols like MQTT, HTTP, and Zigbee define how these devices exchange information. As technology evolves, IoT continues to play a central role in creating intelligent, responsive homes that make life easier and more efficient. In the following chapters, we will explore how to use these IoT sensors and protocols to bring your own smart home projects to life.

CHAPTER 4

ESSENTIAL TOOLS AND COMPONENTS FOR SMART HOMES

Building a smart home requires a range of tools and components to connect and control devices, automate tasks, and collect data. In this chapter, we'll take a close look at the essential components you'll need to get started with your smart home projects, how to select the right tools for different needs, and the power of open-source platforms that make home automation both accessible and customizable.

Overview of Components (Sensors, Relays, Actuators, Motors, etc.)

To turn a regular home into a smart home, various components are involved in sensing, controlling, and automating actions. Let's go over some of the key components:

1. **Sensors** Sensors are devices that detect changes in the environment and gather data that can be

processed by other devices. In smart homes, sensors are used to monitor conditions like temperature, motion, humidity, light, and sound. The data collected by these sensors can trigger actions such as turning on lights, adjusting the thermostat, or sending notifications.

Common sensors used in smart homes:

- o **Temperature and Humidity Sensors (e.g., DHT11/DHT22)**: Used to monitor the indoor climate and control heating or cooling systems.
- o **Motion Sensors (e.g., PIR)**: Detect movement and are often used in security systems to trigger alarms or turn on lights.
- o **Light Sensors**: Measure ambient light levels and are often used to adjust lighting based on natural light.
- o **Gas and Smoke Detectors**: Detect dangerous gases like carbon monoxide or smoke and trigger alarms for safety.
- o **Proximity Sensors**: Used to detect the presence of objects or people, commonly used in smart locks or automatic doors.

2. **Relays** A relay is an electronic switch that can control high-power devices using low-power signals.

Relays are typically used to turn on or off larger devices like fans, lights, or security systems based on input from sensors. They work by controlling the flow of electricity to a device, allowing Raspberry Pi or microcontrollers to control devices without directly powering them.

Common types of relays used in smart homes:

- o **Solid-State Relays (SSR)**: Used for precise control of devices, ideal for applications requiring more reliability and speed.
- o **Mechanical Relays**: Often used in larger systems for their durability and low cost.

3. **Actuators** Actuators are devices that convert signals (usually electrical) into physical movement or action. They are often paired with sensors to automate tasks. For example, when a motion sensor detects movement, an actuator can move a curtain or turn on a fan.

Common types of actuators in smart homes:

- o **Linear Actuators**: Move in a straight line and are used in applications such as automated blinds or smart windows.

    o **Rotary Actuators**: Convert electrical energy into rotational motion, often used in motors for appliances, such as automated doors or smart locks.

4. **Motors** Motors are used to drive mechanical devices in your home, like opening and closing windows, adjusting blinds, or rotating surveillance cameras. In smart homes, motors can be automated to respond to specific events or triggers.

   Types of motors used in home automation:

       o **DC Motors**: Used in applications like curtain motors or small robotic systems.

       o **Stepper Motors**: Precise motors used in more complex automation tasks, like positioning cameras or other moving parts in the home.

5. **Power Supplies** A reliable power supply is essential for ensuring that your devices, sensors, and actuators function correctly. For Raspberry Pi-based projects, a constant power supply is critical, and using regulated power adapters or battery backups ensures that your home automation system runs smoothly even in the event of a power outage.

6. **Communication Modules** Communication modules allow smart home devices to talk to each other over

wireless or wired networks. Some of the most common communication modules for home automation include:

- o **Wi-Fi Modules (e.g., ESP8266, ESP32)**: Allow devices to connect to a home Wi-Fi network and communicate with other devices or cloud-based services.
- o **Bluetooth Modules**: Enable communication between devices in close proximity, ideal for controlling devices like smart locks and speakers.
- o **Zigbee or Z-Wave Modules**: Provide a low-power, long-range solution for connecting a large number of smart devices over a mesh network.

How to Select the Right Tools for Different Smart Home Projects

Choosing the right tools for your smart home project depends on the specific goals, budget, and complexity of the system you're designing. Here are some tips for selecting the appropriate components:

1. **Identify Your Needs**: Start by identifying the specific tasks you want to automate. Do you want to control lighting, monitor security, adjust the climate, or improve energy efficiency? Understanding your

needs will help you determine the sensors, relays, and actuators you need.

2. **Consider Device Compatibility**: Make sure the components you choose are compatible with the system you plan to use. For instance, if you're using Raspberry Pi, make sure your sensors and actuators are compatible with GPIO pins or communication protocols (like MQTT or HTTP).

3. **Understand Power Requirements**: Some sensors and actuators require more power than others. If your system is battery-powered, select low-power devices. Otherwise, consider the availability of power sources and the energy consumption of each component.

4. **Choose Scalable Solutions**: Look for components that can scale as you expand your smart home. For example, Zigbee and Z-Wave allow devices to form a mesh network, which can be expanded as needed without compromising performance.

5. **Budget and Quality**: While it's tempting to go for cheaper components, quality and reliability are essential for long-term use. Sometimes it's better to invest a little more in durable, reliable components to avoid having to replace them frequently.

Introduction to Open-Source Tools and Platforms

One of the biggest advantages of building a smart home using Raspberry Pi and IoT components is the availability of open-source tools and platforms. These tools help you develop, control, and automate your smart home systems without the need for expensive proprietary software. Here are some popular open-source tools that can help streamline your smart home projects:

1. **Home Assistant**: Home Assistant is one of the most popular open-source platforms for home automation. It runs on Raspberry Pi and integrates with thousands of devices and services. With Home Assistant, you can create automation rules, control devices, and visualize your smart home setup through an intuitive web interface. It supports various communication protocols, including MQTT, Zigbee, and Z-Wave.

2. **OpenHAB**: OpenHAB (Open Home Automation Bus) is another powerful open-source platform that supports a wide range of smart home devices. OpenHAB is designed to run on multiple platforms, including Raspberry Pi, and provides flexibility in creating custom rules and automation scripts. It also

integrates with various third-party services and devices.

3. **Node-RED**: Node-RED is a flow-based programming tool that allows you to wire together IoT devices, sensors, and services. It's highly visual, which makes it beginner-friendly, yet it also provides advanced capabilities for more complex automation workflows. It works well with Raspberry Pi and can integrate with a wide range of devices.

4. **Open Source Automation Software Libraries**: There are several Python libraries (such as **RPi.GPIO**, **pigpio**, and **gpiozero**) that allow you to interface with the Raspberry Pi's GPIO pins and control sensors and actuators directly. These libraries are free and can be used to develop custom home automation projects.

5. **MQTT Brokers (e.g., Mosquitto)**: MQTT is an open-source messaging protocol for IoT, and Mosquitto is one of the most widely used MQTT brokers. It helps devices send and receive messages in a lightweight, efficient manner. MQTT is perfect for handling real-time data from sensors and controlling devices in your smart home.

6. **Homebridge**: If you're looking to integrate your Raspberry Pi setup with Apple HomeKit, Homebridge is an open-source platform that makes it possible to connect non-HomeKit devices to Apple's ecosystem. It's a great way to bring additional devices into the Apple Home app.

Conclusion

Creating a smart home requires a variety of tools and components, from sensors and relays to communication modules and power supplies. By understanding the types of components available and selecting the right ones based on your needs, you can ensure your system is both functional and efficient. Leveraging open-source tools and platforms, such as Home Assistant or Node-RED, can further enhance your smart home by providing flexibility, customizability, and cost-effectiveness. These tools make it easier to design and implement intelligent automation that improves comfort, convenience, and security in your home.

CHAPTER 5

SETTING UP YOUR DEVELOPMENT ENVIRONMENT

To start creating a smart home using Raspberry Pi and IoT sensors, you need to set up a development environment that allows you to control devices, process sensor data, and automate tasks. This chapter will guide you through preparing your Raspberry Pi to work with IoT sensors, installing necessary software like Python and Node-RED, and introducing key coding environments and libraries that will help you develop your IoT projects.

Preparing Your Raspberry Pi to Work with IoT Sensors

Before diving into coding, it's essential to ensure that your Raspberry Pi is ready to interface with the various IoT sensors and devices you plan to use in your smart home projects. Here's a step-by-step guide to getting started:

1. **Install Raspberry Pi OS**

- o Ensure that you have Raspberry Pi OS installed on your Raspberry Pi. If you haven't done this yet, you can follow the instructions in Chapter 2 to download and install Raspberry Pi OS using the Raspberry Pi Imager.
- o Once the operating system is installed, boot up the Raspberry Pi and complete the setup process, including Wi-Fi configuration and software updates.

2. **Connect Your Raspberry Pi to the Internet**

- o Connect your Raspberry Pi to your home network either via Wi-Fi or Ethernet. This connection is essential for allowing your Raspberry Pi to communicate with other devices and sensors.
- o Ensure that your Raspberry Pi has a stable internet connection so that you can install software packages and libraries needed for your IoT projects.

3. **Enable GPIO Pins**

- o The General Purpose Input/Output (GPIO) pins on the Raspberry Pi are used to connect various sensors and actuators. You'll need to enable the GPIO interface to control and read from these pins.
- o Open the Raspberry Pi Configuration tool by typing `sudo raspi-config` in the terminal. In

the configuration menu, navigate to **Interfacing Options** and enable the **GPIO**.

4. **Attach IoT Sensors to the Raspberry Pi**

   o Once your Raspberry Pi is set up and the GPIO pins are enabled, you can start connecting IoT sensors (such as temperature, humidity, motion sensors, etc.) to the GPIO pins. Use jumper wires to connect the sensor pins to the appropriate GPIO pins on the Raspberry Pi.

5. **Check for Power Requirements**

   o Ensure that the sensors and devices you're connecting to the Raspberry Pi are powered appropriately. Some sensors may require external power sources, so double-check the specifications of each component to avoid damage.

Installing Necessary Software (Python, Node-RED, etc.)

After preparing the hardware, the next step is to install the software tools that will allow you to interact with your sensors and develop your smart home automation system. The most common software tools for Raspberry Pi and IoT projects are Python, Node-RED, and other associated libraries.

1. **Install Python**
   - Python is the most popular programming language for IoT projects on Raspberry Pi due to its simplicity and versatility. Raspberry Pi OS comes with Python pre-installed, but you can update it to the latest version by running the following commands in the terminal:

   ```sql
   sudo apt update
   sudo apt upgrade
   sudo apt install python3
   ```

   - Python is essential for writing scripts that interact with IoT sensors and automate tasks in your smart home system.

2. **Install Python Libraries for IoT**
   - To interact with the GPIO pins and read sensor data, you will need to install several Python libraries:
     - **RPi.GPIO**: A library that allows you to control the GPIO pins of your Raspberry Pi. To install it, run:

     ```nginx

     ```

```
sudo   apt   install   python3-
rpi.gpio
```

- **gpiozero**: A high-level library for controlling GPIO devices. It is easier to use than RPi.GPIO and supports a wide range of devices, including sensors and motors. Install it by running:

```
nginx
```

```
sudo   apt   install   python3-
gpiozero
```

- **Adafruit_DHT**: A library for reading data from DHT temperature and humidity sensors. You can install it by running:

```
nginx
```

```
pip3 install Adafruit_DHT
```

3. **Install Node-RED**
   o Node-RED is an open-source, flow-based programming tool for wiring together hardware devices, APIs, and online services. It is a powerful tool for building smart home

51

automation systems with a visual interface, and it is commonly used in IoT projects.

o To install Node-RED on your Raspberry Pi, open a terminal and run the following command:

```
nginx
```

```
bash          <(curl          -sL
https://raw.githubusercontent.com/n
ode-red/raspberrypi-
docker/master/install.sh)
```

o After installation, you can start Node-RED by typing:

```
sql
```

```
node-red-start
```

o Once Node-RED is running, you can access the interface by navigating to `http://<Raspberry Pi IP address>:1880` in a web browser. From here, you can create visual flows that control your smart home devices.

4. **Install MQTT Broker (Mosquitto)**

o MQTT (Message Queuing Telemetry Transport) is a lightweight messaging protocol used for communication between IoT devices. To set up

MQTT communication on your Raspberry Pi, you can install the Mosquitto MQTT broker.

o   Install Mosquitto with the following commands:

```
pgsql
```

```
sudo apt update
sudo    apt    install    mosquitto
mosquitto-clients
sudo systemctl enable mosquitto
```

o   Mosquitto allows devices to communicate with each other by publishing and subscribing to messages over MQTT. You can use MQTT to send sensor data or trigger actions based on specific events.

Introduction to Coding Environments and Libraries for IoT Projects

Once your Raspberry Pi is prepared and the necessary software is installed, you can start coding your IoT projects. There are a few different environments and libraries that make IoT development easy, even for beginners.

1. **Python Programming Environment**

- o Python is the most commonly used programming language for Raspberry Pi IoT projects. You can use any text editor or integrated development environment (IDE) to write Python code. Some popular options are:
  - **Thonny**: The default IDE for Python on Raspberry Pi. It's simple and user-friendly, perfect for beginners.
  - **Visual Studio Code**: A more advanced code editor with extensive support for Python and IoT development.
  - **PyCharm**: An IDE specifically designed for Python development, offering a range of useful features like code completion and debugging.
- o Python's syntax is straightforward, and it has a large library of packages that can be used for various IoT tasks, from interacting with hardware to processing sensor data.

2. **Node-RED Development Environment**

- o Node-RED provides a visual environment for building IoT applications. You don't need to write code manually; instead, you use drag-and-drop nodes to create "flows" that define how devices interact with each other.

o Each node represents a function, such as reading a sensor, sending a message, or controlling an actuator. You can wire these nodes together to create automation rules, such as turning on a fan when the temperature exceeds a certain threshold.

3. **Libraries for IoT Projects** There are many Python libraries available to help you get started with IoT projects on Raspberry Pi. Here are some of the most useful ones:

   o **RPi.GPIO**: For controlling Raspberry Pi's GPIO pins.

   o **gpiozero**: A higher-level library for controlling devices connected to GPIO pins.

   o **Adafruit IO**: A cloud service that works with the Adafruit platform for storing and analyzing IoT data.

   o **Paho MQTT**: A Python client library for MQTT messaging.

   o **Flask**: A web framework that allows you to create web interfaces to control your IoT devices.

4. **Web-Based Platforms for IoT** In addition to local tools, there are cloud-based platforms that allow you to monitor, control, and automate your IoT devices. Some of the popular platforms for IoT include:

o **Blynk**: An IoT platform with a mobile app that lets you control devices remotely via a smartphone.

o **ThingSpeak**: A cloud-based platform for IoT data collection and analysis, especially useful for sensor data.

o **Google Cloud IoT**: A powerful platform for managing IoT devices at scale, suitable for more complex projects.

Conclusion

Setting up a development environment for Raspberry Pi and IoT sensors is an essential step in creating your own smart home system. By installing the right software tools—such as Python, Node-RED, and MQTT—you can begin building automation systems that control devices, collect data, and respond to real-time events. With the right coding environments and libraries, you'll be able to tackle a wide variety of IoT projects and bring your smart home ideas to life.

CHAPTER 6

NETWORKING YOUR SMART HOME DEVICES

In a smart home, the ability for devices to communicate with each other is essential for automation and control. This chapter will guide you through the process of connecting IoT devices to your home network, introduce key networking technologies like Wi-Fi, Zigbee, and Bluetooth, and discuss security concerns to ensure your smart home stays safe and secure.

How to Connect IoT Devices to the Home Network

Connecting IoT devices to your home network is the first step in making them part of your smart home ecosystem. There are different ways to connect IoT devices to your network, depending on the type of device and the communication protocol it uses.

1. **Connecting Devices via Wi-Fi**
   o Wi-Fi is the most common method for connecting IoT devices to the home network. Many smart

home devices, such as smart thermostats, cameras, and smart lights, come with built-in Wi-Fi support, allowing them to connect to your home router.

- To connect a device via Wi-Fi:
  - **Set Up Your Router**: Ensure your router is functioning properly and provides stable internet access throughout your home. It's a good idea to set up a dedicated 2.4GHz Wi-Fi network for your IoT devices, as some devices may not support 5GHz Wi-Fi.
  - **Connect the Device**: Follow the manufacturer's instructions to connect the IoT device to your network. This usually involves entering your Wi-Fi network's name (SSID) and password during the device setup process. Some devices may use a smartphone app to guide you through the connection.
  - **Assign Static IPs (Optional)**: For easier management of devices, you might want to assign static IP addresses to key devices, so they always have the same address on the network. This can

simplify automation tasks or troubleshooting.

2. Connecting Devices via Zigbee

o Zigbee is a wireless mesh networking protocol that is used in many smart home devices, such as lights, sensors, and smart plugs. Zigbee networks are known for being low-power and reliable, making them ideal for battery-operated devices.

o Unlike Wi-Fi, Zigbee uses a hub or bridge (such as the **Amazon Echo Plus** or a **Raspberry Pi with a Zigbee USB dongle**) to connect Zigbee devices to the internet. This hub acts as the central communication point for all Zigbee devices.

o **Setting Up Zigbee**:

- Plug in your Zigbee hub and connect it to your Wi-Fi router via Ethernet or Wi-Fi.

- Pair Zigbee devices (like smart bulbs or sensors) to the hub using a mobile app or the device's setup process.

- Once paired, the Zigbee hub will allow your devices to communicate and connect to your home network, making them accessible via smartphone apps or voice assistants.

3. Connecting Devices via Bluetooth

- Bluetooth is another common protocol for connecting smart home devices, especially for shorter-range communication. It's often used in devices like smart locks, smart speakers, and fitness trackers.

- Bluetooth has two versions of communication: **Classic Bluetooth** (used for devices like wireless speakers and audio systems) and **Bluetooth Low Energy (BLE)** (used for low-power, battery-operated devices like smart locks or motion sensors).

- **Setting Up Bluetooth Devices**:

  - Ensure that your Raspberry Pi or smartphone supports Bluetooth communication (you may need a Bluetooth USB dongle for Raspberry Pi).

  - Pair your Bluetooth-enabled device with the Raspberry Pi or smartphone by enabling Bluetooth on both devices and following the pairing process.

  - Once paired, the device can be controlled either via Bluetooth on the Raspberry Pi or using voice assistants like Alexa or Google Assistant, if supported.

Introduction to Wi-Fi, Zigbee, and Bluetooth for IoT

When building a smart home, it's important to choose the right communication protocol to ensure that your devices work together seamlessly. Let's look at the key protocols that power most IoT devices:

1. **Wi-Fi for IoT**
   - o **Strengths**: Wi-Fi offers fast communication and high bandwidth, making it ideal for devices that require a lot of data transfer, such as security cameras or streaming devices. It also provides easy integration with other devices on the home network, including smartphones and voice assistants.
   - o **Limitations**: Wi-Fi can be power-hungry, and because most routers have a limited range, Wi-Fi may not be ideal for low-power, long-range devices like motion sensors. Additionally, network congestion can slow down communication between devices if many Wi-Fi devices are connected.

2. **Zigbee for IoT**
   - o **Strengths**: Zigbee is designed for low-power, low-bandwidth applications, making it perfect for

61

smart home devices that don't require a lot of data transfer, such as light bulbs, sensors, and smart locks. Zigbee's mesh network design means that devices can communicate over greater distances by relaying messages through nearby devices, ensuring reliable communication.

o **Limitations**: Zigbee requires a hub or gateway to connect to your Wi-Fi network and may have limited device compatibility compared to Wi-Fi. However, many smart home ecosystems (like Amazon Alexa and Google Home) support Zigbee through their hubs.

3. **Bluetooth for IoT**

o **Strengths**: Bluetooth is great for short-range, low-power communication, and it is widely used in portable and wearable devices. It's simple to set up, consumes little power, and doesn't require a central hub or internet connection for local communication.

o **Limitations**: Bluetooth's range is relatively short (typically up to 100 meters), and it's not suitable for high-bandwidth applications. It may not be ideal for devices that need to communicate over longer distances or with high data transfer rates.

Security Concerns with IoT Networks and Best Practices

While IoT devices offer immense convenience, they also introduce security risks. Many IoT devices have internet connectivity, which means they can be vulnerable to cyberattacks. Securing your IoT network is essential to protect your privacy and prevent unauthorized access to your devices.

1. **Common IoT Security Risks**
   - **Weak Passwords**: Many IoT devices come with default usernames and passwords that are easy to guess or find online. Attackers can exploit these weak credentials to gain unauthorized access to your devices.
   - **Unencrypted Communication**: Without encryption, the data transmitted between IoT devices can be intercepted, allowing hackers to eavesdrop on or manipulate communication.
   - **Outdated Firmware**: IoT devices that don't receive regular firmware updates are vulnerable to security holes. Exploits in outdated devices can give attackers control over your devices or expose sensitive information.

o **Lack of Network Segmentation**: IoT devices that are connected to the same network as computers or smartphones can potentially give attackers access to other devices on the network if one device is compromised.

2. **Best Practices for Securing Your IoT Network**

o **Change Default Credentials**: Always change the default username and password on IoT devices to something strong and unique. Use a password manager to generate and store complex passwords.

o **Use Encryption**: Ensure that devices use encrypted communication (such as TLS/SSL for HTTP or encryption for MQTT). This prevents eavesdropping and tampering with data.

o **Enable Two-Factor Authentication (2FA)**: For devices and services that support it, enable two-factor authentication to add an extra layer of protection.

o **Keep Devices Up-to-Date**: Regularly check for firmware updates for all your IoT devices. Install updates as soon as they become available to patch any security vulnerabilities.

o **Segment Your Network**: Create a separate Wi-Fi network for your IoT devices. This will prevent attackers from accessing your computers, smartphones, or other critical devices in case one of your IoT devices is compromised.

o **Use a Firewall**: Set up a firewall to monitor and control the traffic that enters or leaves your network. Firewalls can block suspicious connections and protect your IoT devices from external threats.

3. **Monitor and Audit IoT Devices**

o Regularly monitor your IoT devices to ensure they are operating as expected. Use network monitoring tools to identify unusual activity or unauthorized access attempts.

o Many IoT platforms and devices offer audit logs that track device activity. Review these logs periodically to spot any signs of potential security breaches.

Conclusion

Networking your smart home devices is the foundation of any home automation system. By using Wi-Fi, Zigbee, or Bluetooth, you can connect various devices and create a seamless, interconnected environment. However, security must be a priority when designing your IoT network. Following best practices like changing default passwords, using encryption, and regularly updating firmware will help protect your devices from vulnerabilities and ensure that your smart home remains secure. With the right network setup and security measures, you can enjoy the convenience of smart home automation without compromising on safety.

CHAPTER 7

WORKING WITH TEMPERATURE AND HUMIDITY SENSORS

Temperature and humidity sensors are essential components of any smart home, allowing you to monitor and control the indoor climate for comfort, energy efficiency, and health. In this chapter, we will walk through the setup process for the DHT11 and DHT22 sensors, which are commonly used in smart home automation projects. We'll also explore how these sensors can be used to automate air conditioning and heating based on environmental conditions.

Step-by-Step Guide to Setting Up DHT11/DHT22 Temperature and Humidity Sensors

The DHT11 and DHT22 sensors are both low-cost, reliable, and widely used for measuring temperature and humidity. The primary difference between the two is that the DHT22 offers better accuracy and a wider temperature range than the DHT11. Both sensors work similarly, and setting them up with your Raspberry Pi or microcontroller is straightforward.

Components Needed:

- **DHT11 or DHT22 sensor**
- **Raspberry Pi** (or any compatible microcontroller like Arduino)
- **4.7kΩ resistor** (used to pull the data line high)
- **Breadboard** and **jumper wires**
- **Python or Node-RED software** (to read sensor data)

Wiring the Sensor to Raspberry Pi

1. **Connect the DHT11/DHT22 Sensor to the Raspberry Pi:**
   - **VCC**: Connect the **VCC pin** of the sensor to a 3.3V or 5V pin on the Raspberry Pi (depending on the sensor model). The DHT11 works with 3.3V, while the DHT22 can work with both 3.3V and 5V.
   - **GND**: Connect the **GND pin** of the sensor to a GND pin on the Raspberry Pi.
   - **Data Pin**: Connect the **Data pin** of the sensor to one of the GPIO pins on the Raspberry Pi. For example, you can use GPIO 17.
   - **Resistor**: Place the **4.7kΩ resistor** between the **VCC pin** and the **Data pin** to stabilize the signal and ensure proper communication.

2. **Verify the Connections**: Double-check your wiring to ensure that all connections are secure and correctly placed on the breadboard and Raspberry Pi.

Installing Necessary Software

Before reading data from the DHT sensor, you'll need to install the necessary Python libraries for interfacing with the sensor.

1. **Install the Adafruit DHT Python Library:** The easiest way to interface with the DHT11/DHT22 sensor is by using the **Adafruit DHT** library. You can install it by opening the terminal on your Raspberry Pi and running the following commands:

```sql
sql

sudo apt update
sudo apt install python3-pip
sudo pip3 install Adafruit_DHT
```

2. **Test the Sensor**: After the library is installed, you can test your sensor by running a simple Python script to read temperature and humidity data. Here's a basic example:

```python
python

import Adafruit_DHT

# Set sensor type and GPIO pin
sensor = Adafruit_DHT.DHT22  # Use DHT11 if
you're using the DHT11 sensor
pin = 17  # GPIO pin number where the sensor
is connected

# Read the humidity and temperature
humidity,           temperature           =
Adafruit_DHT.read_retry(sensor, pin)

if humidity is not None and temperature is
not None:
    print(f'Temperature:
{temperature:.1f}°C                Humidity:
{humidity:.1f}%')
else:
    print('Failed to get reading. Try
again!')
```

3. **Run the Script**: Save the script and run it. You should see the temperature and humidity readings displayed on the terminal. If everything is connected correctly, the data will be displayed in real-time.

Real-World Application: Automating Air Conditioning and Heating Based on Environmental Conditions

Now that you can read the temperature and humidity data from your sensor, let's explore how to use this data to automate your air conditioning and heating systems.

The Goal

We'll create a system that automatically adjusts the temperature inside your home based on certain thresholds, turning the air conditioning or heating system on or off as needed. This will not only ensure comfort but also save energy by preventing unnecessary operation of HVAC systems.

Components Needed:

- **Temperature and Humidity Sensors (DHT11 or DHT22)**
- **Relay Module**: To control the power of the air conditioning/heating unit.
- **Smart plug** or **IR remote controller**: To control the HVAC system (optional, if you're using a non-smart HVAC system).

- **Raspberry Pi or microcontroller**: To process sensor data and control the relay.

Wiring the Relay to Raspberry Pi

1. **Connect the Relay Module**:
   - Connect the **VCC** pin of the relay to the 5V pin on the Raspberry Pi.
   - Connect the **GND** pin of the relay to a ground pin on the Raspberry Pi.
   - Connect the **IN** pin of the relay to one of the GPIO pins on the Raspberry Pi (for example, GPIO 18). This pin will be used to control the relay.

2. **Connect the Air Conditioning/Heating System**:
   - Depending on the type of HVAC system you're using, you'll need a relay capable of handling the power requirements. A smart plug with relay control can be used to switch on/off your air conditioning or heating.
   - Ensure that the relay is correctly wired to control the power flow to your HVAC system.

Setting Temperature Thresholds and Automating Control

Let's write a Python script that reads the temperature data and compares it to a set threshold. If the temperature exceeds or falls below the threshold, the air conditioning or heating will be triggered.

Here's a simple script that automates temperature control:

```python
import Adafruit_DHT
import RPi.GPIO as GPIO
import time

# Set sensor and GPIO pin
sensor = Adafruit_DHT.DHT22
pin = 17  # GPIO pin connected to DHT sensor
relay_pin = 18  # GPIO pin connected to relay

# Set the temperature thresholds (in Celsius)
min_temp = 18    # Minimum temperature (for heating)
max_temp = 24    # Maximum temperature (for cooling)

# Setup GPIO
GPIO.setmode(GPIO.BCM)
GPIO.setup(relay_pin, GPIO.OUT)

# Function to control HVAC
def control_hvac(temp):
    if temp < min_temp:
```

```
        print(f"Temperature is {temp}°C. Turning
on heating system.")
        GPIO.output(relay_pin,   GPIO.HIGH)    #
Turn on heating
    elif temp > max_temp:
        print(f"Temperature is {temp}°C. Turning
on cooling system.")
        GPIO.output(relay_pin,   GPIO.HIGH)    #
Turn on cooling
    else:
        print(f"Temperature is {temp}°C. No need
to adjust.")
        GPIO.output(relay_pin, GPIO.LOW)  # Turn
off HVAC


# Main loop
try:
    while True:
        humidity,         temperature        =
Adafruit_DHT.read_retry(sensor, pin)

        if humidity is not None and temperature
is not None:
            print(f'Temperature:
{temperature:.1f}°C  Humidity: {humidity:.1f}%')
            control_hvac(temperature)
        else:
            print('Failed  to  get  reading.  Try
again!')
```

```
    time.sleep(10)   # Wait for 10 seconds
before reading again
except KeyboardInterrupt:
    GPIO.cleanup()  # Clean up GPIO on exit
```

Explanation of the Code:

- **Thresholds**: The script checks the current temperature and compares it to the `min_temp` and `max_temp` values. If the temperature is below `min_temp`, it triggers the heating system by activating the relay. If the temperature is above `max_temp`, it triggers the cooling system.
- **Relay Control**: The relay is controlled via GPIO. When the temperature exceeds the thresholds, the relay will turn on the heating or cooling system (depending on the setup).

Conclusion

By using temperature and humidity sensors like the DHT11/DHT22, you can automate your HVAC system based on environmental conditions in your home. This not only enhances comfort but also helps save energy by preventing overuse of air conditioning and heating. Through simple scripts and the power of Raspberry Pi, you can easily build a smart system that adapts to changing temperatures, ensuring that your home stays at the perfect temperature without manual intervention.

CHAPTER 8

LIGHT AND MOTION SENSORS: CREATING AN AUTOMATED LIGHTING SYSTEM

Light and motion sensors are key components of a smart home, enabling the automation of lighting systems based on room occupancy or ambient light levels. In this chapter, we'll explore how to set up and use **PIR (Passive Infrared) motion sensors** to automate lighting based on occupancy, and we'll discuss how these sensors can contribute to energy-saving techniques in your home.

How to Set Up and Use Motion Sensors (PIR)

Motion sensors, particularly PIR sensors, are widely used in smart home systems for detecting movement in a room or area. These sensors use infrared technology to detect body heat or changes in infrared light, triggering an action when motion is detected.

Components Needed:

- **PIR Motion Sensor**: This is the sensor that detects movement.
- **Raspberry Pi** (or any compatible microcontroller like Arduino).
- **Relay Module**: To control the lighting (if you're using a non-smart bulb or light).
- **Breadboard and Jumper Wires**: For connections.
- **Light Bulb** (optional): A regular bulb or a smart bulb that can be controlled.
- **Power Source**: To power your Raspberry Pi and connected devices.

Wiring the PIR Sensor to Raspberry Pi

1. **Connect the PIR Sensor to the Raspberry Pi**:
   - **VCC Pin**: Connect to the 5V or 3.3V pin on the Raspberry Pi (depending on the sensor model).
   - **GND Pin**: Connect to a ground (GND) pin on the Raspberry Pi.
   - **OUT Pin**: Connect to one of the GPIO pins (for example, GPIO 17). This pin will output a HIGH signal when motion is detected and a LOW signal when no motion is detected.

2. **Connect the Relay to the Raspberry Pi (for controlling lighting)**:

- ○ **VCC Pin**: Connect to the 5V pin on the Raspberry Pi.
- ○ **GND Pin**: Connect to a ground pin on the Raspberry Pi.
- ○ **IN Pin**: Connect to another GPIO pin (e.g., GPIO 18) to control the relay, which will turn the light on or off based on motion detection.

Testing the PIR Sensor

Once everything is wired up, you can test the PIR sensor by running a simple Python script to monitor motion detection.

```python
import RPi.GPIO as GPIO
import time

# Set GPIO mode
GPIO.setmode(GPIO.BCM)

# Set up the GPIO pins
PIR_PIN = 17  # PIR motion sensor pin
LED_PIN = 18  # Light control pin (for the relay)

# Set up the PIR sensor and relay pin
GPIO.setup(PIR_PIN, GPIO.IN)
GPIO.setup(LED_PIN, GPIO.OUT)
```

```
try:
    print("Motion           detection           system
initialized.")
    print("Waiting for motion...")
    while True:
        if GPIO.input(PIR_PIN):
            print("Motion detected!")
            GPIO.output(LED_PIN, GPIO.HIGH)    #
Turn on light
        else:
            print("No motion.")
            GPIO.output(LED_PIN, GPIO.LOW)     #
Turn off light
        time.sleep(1)  # Check every second
except KeyboardInterrupt:
    print("Program interrupted.")
    GPIO.cleanup()  # Clean up GPIO on exit
```

Explanation of the Code:

- The **GPIO pins** are set up for both the PIR motion sensor and the relay controlling the light.
- The script continuously checks the **PIR sensor** for motion. If motion is detected, the light (via the relay) is turned on, and if no motion is detected, the light is turned off.
- The loop checks for motion every second, and you can adjust the timing as needed.

Automating Lighting Based on Room Occupancy

One of the most practical applications of PIR motion sensors is automating lighting based on room occupancy. This ensures that lights are only on when needed, improving convenience and saving energy.

How It Works:

- **When the room is occupied**, the motion sensor detects movement and triggers the lights to turn on.
- **When the room is empty**, the motion sensor detects no movement and turns off the lights after a set period of inactivity (e.g., 5 minutes).

This automated system helps reduce energy waste by ensuring that lights are not left on unnecessarily.

Enhancing the System with Timers

To avoid the lights turning off immediately after motion stops (in case of temporary pauses), you can introduce a **delay timer** that keeps the lights on for a certain amount of time after the last motion is detected.

Here's an example modification of the script that includes a timer to keep the lights on for 5 minutes after the last motion is detected:

```python
import RPi.GPIO as GPIO
import time

# Set GPIO mode
GPIO.setmode(GPIO.BCM)

# Set up the GPIO pins
PIR_PIN = 17  # PIR motion sensor pin
LED_PIN = 18  # Light control pin (for the relay)
TIMEOUT = 300  # Time in seconds to keep the light
on after no motion (5 minutes)

# Set up the PIR sensor and relay pin
GPIO.setup(PIR_PIN, GPIO.IN)
GPIO.setup(LED_PIN, GPIO.OUT)

last_motion_time = time.time()

try:
    print("Motion          detection          system
initialized.")
    print("Waiting for motion...")
    while True:
```

```
    if GPIO.input(PIR_PIN):
        print("Motion detected!")
        GPIO.output(LED_PIN, GPIO.HIGH)     #
Turn on light
        last_motion_time = time.time()     #
Update the last motion time
    else:
        print("No motion.")
        # Check if the light should be turned
off after timeout period
        if time.time() - last_motion_time >
TIMEOUT:
            print("No motion for 5 minutes.
Turning off the light.")
            GPIO.output(LED_PIN, GPIO.LOW)
# Turn off light
    time.sleep(1)  # Check every second
except KeyboardInterrupt:
    print("Program interrupted.")
    GPIO.cleanup()  # Clean up GPIO on exit
```

Explanation:

- This version of the script includes a **TIMEOUT** variable that specifies how long to keep the light on after the last motion was detected. After this timeout period, the light turns off if no further motion is detected.

Energy-Saving Techniques Using Light and Motion Sensors

Motion and light sensors can significantly contribute to energy savings in a smart home system. Here are a few techniques for leveraging these sensors to reduce energy consumption:

1. **Automated Lighting Control**: By turning lights on only when needed (i.e., when motion is detected) and turning them off when the room is empty, you can save energy that would otherwise be wasted by leaving lights on.

2. **Daylight Harvesting**: Combine light sensors with motion sensors to create a daylight harvesting system. This means that the lights are automatically dimmed or turned off when there is enough natural light coming into the room, reducing the need for artificial lighting during the day.

   For example, a **light sensor** can measure the ambient light level, and if it's above a certain threshold (indicating sufficient daylight), the system can turn off or dim the artificial lights.

3. **Customizable Occupancy Times**: Set different timeout periods for various rooms depending on usage patterns. For example, lights in the living room may stay on for longer periods after motion stops, while lights in less frequently used spaces (like the garage or hallway) may have shorter timeouts, ensuring they turn off quickly.

4. **Integration with Other Smart Systems**: Motion sensors can be integrated with other systems in your home, such as HVAC systems or window blinds. For instance, if motion is detected in a room, the system can adjust the thermostat to a comfortable temperature, ensuring efficient energy use.

Conclusion

Using PIR motion sensors and light sensors to automate lighting in your smart home is an excellent way to save energy and improve convenience. By setting up motion sensors to detect occupancy and control the lights accordingly, you can ensure that lights are only on when needed. Additionally, combining motion sensors with light sensors can lead to even greater energy savings, especially when employing techniques like daylight harvesting and adjustable occupancy timers. With a few simple automation rules, you can reduce energy waste while keeping your home comfortable and well-lit.

CHAPTER 9

BUILDING A SMART DOORBELL SYSTEM

A smart doorbell system is one of the most practical and popular home automation projects. By adding a camera, video streaming, and remote control features, you can monitor visitors, speak to them, and receive notifications—all from your smartphone or computer. In this chapter, we'll guide you through building your own smart doorbell system using Raspberry Pi, integrating it with a camera for video streaming, and setting up remote control and notifications.

Step-by-Step Instructions for Building a Smart Doorbell with a Camera

Before you start, here's a list of the essential components you'll need for the smart doorbell system:

Components Needed:

- **Raspberry Pi** (Raspberry Pi 3/4 is ideal)
- **Raspberry Pi Camera Module** (or a compatible USB webcam)

- **Push button** (to trigger the doorbell)
- **Relay Module** (for controlling the button or triggering the doorbell sound)
- **Speaker** (for the doorbell sound)
- **Microphone** (for communication with visitors, optional)
- **Internet connection** (Wi-Fi or Ethernet)
- **Power Supply** (for Raspberry Pi)

Wiring the Camera, Button, and Speaker to Raspberry Pi

1. **Camera Module**:
   - If you're using the official **Raspberry Pi Camera Module**, connect it to the **CSI port** on the Raspberry Pi. The camera module plugs directly into the Raspberry Pi and requires no additional power source. Ensure the ribbon cable is inserted correctly into the port.

2. **Push Button**:
   - Connect the **push button** to a **GPIO pin** on the Raspberry Pi. When the button is pressed, it will trigger an event (such as taking a picture, starting the video feed, or sending a notification). Connect one pin of the button to a **GPIO pin** (for example, GPIO 17), and the other to **ground (GND)**.

3. **Speaker and Microphone**:

- o If you want to add a two-way communication feature, you can connect a **USB microphone** and **USB speaker** to the Raspberry Pi. These components will allow you to speak with visitors through the system.

- o For the doorbell sound, you can use an external speaker connected via the 3.5mm audio jack or a USB speaker.

4. **Relay Module (Optional)**:

- o If you want the system to trigger an external device, such as a chime or a light when the button is pressed, use a **relay module**. The relay can be connected to the button press input, which can trigger the relay to activate the doorbell sound or activate other features.

Setting Up the Raspberry Pi and Camera

1. **Install the Operating System**:

- o If you haven't already, install **Raspberry Pi OS** on your Raspberry Pi (instructions in previous chapters). Make sure your Raspberry Pi is connected to the internet and fully updated.

2. **Enable the Camera Interface**:

- o Open the **Raspberry Pi Configuration** tool (from the desktop interface or by typing `sudo raspi-config` in the terminal).

- o Go to **Interfacing Options**, select **Camera**, and enable it. This will allow you to use the camera module with your Raspberry Pi.

3. **Install Camera Software**:
   - o You can use **motionEyeOS** or other open-source software like **MJPG-Streamer** to handle video streaming. Here's how to set up **MJPG-Streamer**:
     - Open the terminal and install the MJPG-Streamer package:

```sql
sql
```

```
sudo apt update
sudo apt install mjpg-streamer
```

     - Connect your camera to the Raspberry Pi and use the following command to start the video stream:

```nginx
nginx
```

```
mjpg_streamer            -i
"/usr/local/lib/mjpg-
streamer/input_raspicam.so" -o
"/usr/local/lib/mjpg-
streamer/output_http.so      -w
```

```
/usr/local/lib/mjpg-
streamer/www"
```

- This will start streaming the video from
  the camera on the Pi, and you can access
  it via your browser by navigating to the
  Raspberry Pi's IP address followed by
  port 8080 (e.g., `http://<your-pi-ip>:8080`).

Integrating with Raspberry Pi and Basic Video Streaming

Once you have your camera module and Raspberry Pi set up, you can integrate the video streaming functionality into your smart doorbell system. The goal is to capture video when the doorbell button is pressed and stream the video to a mobile device or computer.

Video Streaming Setup with MJPG-Streamer

1. **Start the Video Stream**: As mentioned, you can use **MJPG-Streamer** for video streaming. To make the video accessible from a web browser, ensure that you have the Raspberry Pi's IP address.

2. **Customizing the Stream**: To adjust the resolution or frame rate of the video feed, you can modify the command as follows:

```
nginx
```

```
mjpg_streamer  -i  "/usr/local/lib/mjpg-
streamer/input_raspicam.so -x 640 -y 480 -
fps  30"  -o  "/usr/local/lib/mjpg-
streamer/output_http.so          -w
/usr/local/lib/mjpg-streamer/www"
```

This sets the video resolution to 640x480 pixels and 30 frames per second, ideal for smooth video streaming.

Display the Video Feed on Your Smartphone or Computer

You can view the live video stream from your Raspberry Pi's camera on a mobile phone or computer via a web browser. Simply type the IP address of your Raspberry Pi followed by port 8080 (e.g., http://<Raspberry_Pi_IP>:8080) to view the feed.

For more advanced functionality, such as storing videos or integrating with other smart home platforms, you may choose to use software like **Home Assistant** or **OpenHAB**, which can integrate video feeds, notifications, and alerts into one unified smart home interface.

Remote Control and Notifications

A smart doorbell system isn't just about seeing who's at the door—it's also about interacting with visitors and getting notifications when someone presses the button. Here's how you can implement these features.

Remote Notifications with Pushbullet or Pushover

To receive notifications on your smartphone or computer when someone presses the doorbell button, you can use a notification service like **Pushbullet** or **Pushover**.

1. **Set Up Pushbullet**:
    o First, sign up for a **Pushbullet** account and create an API key from the settings page.
    o Install the **Pushbullet** Python library on your Raspberry Pi by running:

```
nginx
```

```
pip install pushbullet.py
```

o Write a Python script to send a notification when the doorbell button is pressed:

python

```python
import RPi.GPIO as GPIO
import time
from pushbullet import Pushbullet

# Set GPIO mode and pin
GPIO.setmode(GPIO.BCM)
BUTTON_PIN = 17
GPIO.setup(BUTTON_PIN, GPIO.IN)

# Set up Pushbullet API
pb                           =
Pushbullet("YOUR_PUSHBULLET_API_KEY
")

def send_notification():
    push    =    pb.push_note("Smart
Doorbell", "Someone is at the door!")

try:
    while True:
        if GPIO.input(BUTTON_PIN):
            print("Doorbell
pressed!")
```

```
            send_notification()      #
Send notification
                time.sleep(1)             #
Debounce the button
            time.sleep(0.1)      #  Check
every 100ms
        except KeyboardInterrupt:
        GPIO.cleanup()
```

2. **Push Notifications**:

   o This script will send a push notification to your smartphone whenever the button is pressed. You can install the **Pushbullet** app on your phone to receive these notifications in real-time.

Remote Access to Video Stream

You can also enable remote access to your camera feed, allowing you to see the video feed from anywhere. Using MJPG-Streamer (as mentioned earlier), you can access the stream via your web browser using the IP address and port of your Raspberry Pi.

For more secure remote access, you can configure a **VPN** (Virtual Private Network) or use a **cloud-based platform** to connect your Raspberry Pi to the internet securely.

Conclusion

Building a smart doorbell system with Raspberry Pi, a camera, and motion detection capabilities is a fantastic way to enhance the security and convenience of your home. By following these steps, you can create a system that notifies you when someone presses the doorbell, streams video to your devices, and even allows you to interact with visitors remotely. This project can easily be expanded to include additional features like two-way audio, facial recognition, or integration with other smart home systems.

CHAPTER 10

SMART SECURITY SYSTEMS WITH IOT SENSORS

A smart security system is an integral part of a modern smart home. It enables you to monitor and protect your home using IoT sensors, cameras, and automation. This chapter will guide you through setting up essential security components like **motion detectors**, **door/window sensors**, and **cameras** using Raspberry Pi. You'll also learn how to automate alerts for potential threats and use Raspberry Pi for video surveillance.

Setting Up Motion Detectors, Door/Window Sensors, and Cameras for Security

Creating a smart security system involves using a combination of sensors and cameras to monitor various entry points and areas around your home. These sensors work together to detect movement or unauthorized access and trigger actions like sending notifications or activating alarms.

1. Setting Up Motion Detectors (PIR Sensors)

Motion detectors, often using **PIR (Passive Infrared) sensors**, detect changes in infrared radiation, which is typically caused by moving objects, such as a person walking by. These are often used for triggering alarms, lights, or cameras when movement is detected.

Components Needed:

- **PIR Motion Sensor**
- **Raspberry Pi** or any compatible microcontroller
- **Relay Module** (optional, for controlling alarms or other devices)

Wiring the PIR Sensor:

- Connect the **VCC** pin of the PIR sensor to a 5V or 3.3V pin on the Raspberry Pi.
- Connect the **GND** pin to a ground (GND) pin on the Raspberry Pi.
- Connect the **OUT** pin to a GPIO pin (e.g., GPIO 17) on the Raspberry Pi to detect motion.

Python Script for Motion Detection:

```python

import RPi.GPIO as GPIO
```

```
import time

# Set GPIO mode and pin
GPIO.setmode(GPIO.BCM)
PIR_PIN = 17  # GPIO pin connected to PIR sensor
GPIO.setup(PIR_PIN, GPIO.IN)

try:
    print("Motion          detection          system
initialized.")
    while True:
        if GPIO.input(PIR_PIN):
            print("Motion detected!")
            # Trigger alarm or activate another
device
        else:
            print("No motion detected.")
        time.sleep(1)  # Check every second
except KeyboardInterrupt:
    print("Program interrupted.")
    GPIO.cleanup()
```

This simple script will detect motion using the PIR sensor. You can expand this to trigger cameras or send notifications.

2. Setting Up Door/Window Sensors

Door/window sensors are typically used to monitor the status of doors and windows. They are equipped with a magnetic reed switch that opens or closes when the door or window is opened or closed. This information can be sent to a Raspberry Pi for further action.

Components Needed:

- **Magnetic Reed Switch** (door/window sensor)
- **Raspberry Pi** or microcontroller
- **Relay Module** (optional)

Wiring the Door/Window Sensor:

- Connect the **NO (Normally Open)** pin of the reed switch to a GPIO pin (e.g., GPIO 18).
- Connect the other pin of the reed switch to **ground**.

Python Script for Monitoring Door/Window Status:

python

```python
import RPi.GPIO as GPIO
import time

# Set GPIO mode and pin
GPIO.setmode(GPIO.BCM)
DOOR_PIN = 18  # GPIO pin connected to reed switch
GPIO.setup(DOOR_PIN, GPIO.IN)

try:
```

```
    print("Door/window sensor initialized.")
    while True:
        if GPIO.input(DOOR_PIN):
            print("Door/window is closed.")
        else:
            print("Door/window is open!")
            # Trigger alarm or notification here
        time.sleep(1)
except KeyboardInterrupt:
    print("Program interrupted.")
    GPIO.cleanup()
```

This script will monitor whether a door or window is open and can be expanded to send notifications or trigger alarms.

3. Setting Up Security Cameras

Cameras are critical for a complete security system, allowing you to visually monitor activity around your home. You can integrate a camera with Raspberry Pi for live video streaming and surveillance.

Components Needed:

- **Raspberry Pi Camera Module** (or a USB camera)
- **Raspberry Pi**
- **Internet connection** (for remote access)

Connecting the Camera to Raspberry Pi:

- Attach the **Raspberry Pi Camera Module** to the **CSI port** on the Raspberry Pi (if using the official camera module).
- Enable the camera interface in the Raspberry Pi configuration tool (`sudo raspi-config`), under **Interfacing Options** > **Camera**.

Setting Up Video Streaming:

To stream live video from the Raspberry Pi, you can use **MJPG-Streamer**. Follow these steps to set it up:

1. Install MJPG-Streamer:

```sql
sudo apt update
sudo apt install mjpg-streamer
```

2. Start video streaming using the following command:

```nginx
mjpg_streamer -i "/usr/local/lib/mjpg-streamer/input_raspicam.so" -o "/usr/local/lib/mjpg-
```

```
streamer/output_http.so                    -w
/usr/local/lib/mjpg-streamer/www"
```

3. Access the video stream by navigating to your Raspberry Pi's IP address and port `8080` in your web browser, e.g., `http://<your-pi-ip>:8080`.

How to Automate Alerts and Notifications for Potential Threats

With your sensors and cameras set up, the next step is to automate alerts and notifications to inform you about potential security threats. Here are a few ways to do this:

1. Automating Alerts with Email or Push Notifications

Using services like **Pushbullet** or **Pushover**, you can send alerts when motion is detected or when a door or window is opened. Here's an example of integrating **Pushbullet** for motion alerts:

Install Pushbullet Library:
bash

```
pip install pushbullet.py
```
Python Script for Sending Push Notifications:
python

```python
from pushbullet import Pushbullet
import RPi.GPIO as GPIO
import time

# Pushbullet setup
pb = Pushbullet("YOUR_PUSHBULLET_API_KEY")

# GPIO setup for PIR sensor
GPIO.setmode(GPIO.BCM)
PIR_PIN = 17  # GPIO pin connected to PIR sensor
GPIO.setup(PIR_PIN, GPIO.IN)

def send_alert():
    pb.push_note("Motion     Alert",     "Motion
detected at your door!")

try:
    print("Motion     detection     system
initialized.")
    while True:
        if GPIO.input(PIR_PIN):
            print("Motion detected!")
            send_alert()  # Send notification
        time.sleep(1)
except KeyboardInterrupt:
    print("Program interrupted.")
    GPIO.cleanup()
```

This script will send a **Pushbullet** notification to your phone whenever motion is detected.

2. Automating Camera Capture and Recording

You can set up your security cameras to automatically capture images or record video when motion is detected. This can be done by triggering the camera to start recording when the PIR sensor detects movement.

Example of Camera Trigger:
python

```python
import time
import picamera

# Set up the camera
camera = picamera.PICamera()

# Set up the PIR motion sensor
PIR_PIN = 17
GPIO.setup(PIR_PIN, GPIO.IN)

def capture_image():
    timestamp = time.strftime("%Y%m%d-%H%M%S")

camera.capture(f"/home/pi/security_image_{timestamp}.jpg")
```

```
    print(f"Image                    captured:
security_image_{timestamp}.jpg")

try:
    while True:
        if GPIO.input(PIR_PIN):
            print("Motion detected!")
            capture_image()   # Capture image on
motion detection
        time.sleep(1)
except KeyboardInterrupt:
    camera.close()
    GPIO.cleanup()
```

This script captures an image every time motion is detected
and saves it with a timestamp for easy reference.

Using Raspberry Pi for Video Surveillance Systems

You can integrate video surveillance functionality into your
smart security system by using Raspberry Pi to record video
and stream it to your devices. With tools like **MJPG-
Streamer** or **MotionEyeOS**, you can easily set up a video
surveillance system that allows you to monitor live footage
from your smartphone or computer.

1. Setting Up MotionEyeOS for Surveillance

MotionEyeOS is an open-source software that turns your Raspberry Pi into a powerful video surveillance system. You can install it on your Raspberry Pi and use it to control multiple cameras and access live video feeds remotely.

- Install **MotionEyeOS** onto an SD card using the official instructions from the MotionEye website.
- Boot up the Raspberry Pi with MotionEyeOS, connect it to your network, and access the web interface by entering the Raspberry Pi's IP address into your browser.

2. Recording Video and Storing Data

You can configure your system to automatically record video when motion is detected. MotionEyeOS supports **motion-triggered recording**, and it allows you to store the footage locally on the Raspberry Pi or in the cloud.

Conclusion

Building a smart security system using IoT sensors and Raspberry Pi is an effective way to enhance the safety of your home. By combining motion detectors, door/window sensors, and cameras, you can monitor your home and automate alerts for potential threats. Using tools like **MJPG-Streamer** or **MotionEyeOS**, you can set up a comprehensive video surveillance system that offers real-time streaming and recording capabilities. With automated notifications

CHAPTER 11

AUTOMATING SMART LIGHTS

Automating lighting in a smart home is one of the most common and practical applications of IoT technology. By using IoT sensors and Raspberry Pi, you can automate your lighting based on environmental conditions or triggers. In this chapter, we will explore how to use IoT sensors with Raspberry Pi to control lighting, introduce color-changing LEDs and dimming functionality, and show how to integrate these systems with popular voice assistants like Google Assistant and Alexa.

How to Use IoT Sensors and Raspberry Pi to Control Lighting

Raspberry Pi, combined with IoT sensors, can automate your lighting by detecting factors such as occupancy, ambient light levels, or time of day. For example, lights can automatically turn on when you enter a room, adjust based on the available natural light, or turn off after a set period of inactivity.

Components Needed:

- **Raspberry Pi** (3 or 4)
- **PIR Motion Sensor** (for detecting occupancy)
- **Light Bulb or LED Strip** (for controlling light)
- **Relay Module** (if using a regular bulb)
- **Breadboard and Jumper Wires**
- **Power Supply** (for Raspberry Pi and lights)

Wiring the Motion Sensor and Relay

1. **PIR Motion Sensor**:
   o Connect the **VCC** pin of the PIR sensor to a 5V or 3.3V pin on the Raspberry Pi.
   o Connect the **GND** pin to a ground (GND) pin on the Raspberry Pi.
   o Connect the **OUT** pin to a GPIO pin (e.g., GPIO 17) to detect motion.

2. **Relay Module for Light Control**:
   o Connect the **VCC** pin of the relay to the 5V pin on the Raspberry Pi.
   o Connect the **GND** pin of the relay to a ground (GND) pin on the Raspberry Pi.
   o Connect the **IN** pin of the relay to another GPIO pin (e.g., GPIO 18) to control the relay.

3. **Light Bulb**:

o   If you're using a **regular light bulb**, connect the relay's output to the bulb, ensuring that the relay can handle the voltage and current of the bulb.

o   If you're using a **smart bulb** (like a Wi-Fi-enabled LED bulb), you can skip the relay and connect the bulb directly to the Wi-Fi network.

Python Script for Automating Lighting with PIR Sensor

Here's an example of how you can write a Python script that turns the light on when motion is detected:

```python
python

import RPi.GPIO as GPIO
import time

# Set GPIO mode and pins
GPIO.setmode(GPIO.BCM)
PIR_PIN = 17   # GPIO pin for PIR sensor
RELAY_PIN = 18   # GPIO pin for relay control
GPIO.setup(PIR_PIN, GPIO.IN)   # Set up PIR sensor
pin as input
GPIO.setup(RELAY_PIN, GPIO.OUT)   # Set up relay
pin as output

try:
    print("Waiting for motion...")
    while True:
```

```
if GPIO.input(PIR_PIN):
        print("Motion detected! Turning on
the light.")
            GPIO.output(RELAY_PIN, GPIO.HIGH)  #
Turn on light
        else:
            print("No motion detected. Turning
off the light.")
            GPIO.output(RELAY_PIN, GPIO.LOW)  #
Turn off light
        time.sleep(1)  # Check every second
except KeyboardInterrupt:
    GPIO.cleanup()  # Clean up GPIO on exit
```

In this example, the light will automatically turn on when motion is detected and turn off when there's no motion for a set period.

Introduction to Color-Changing LEDs and Dimming Functionality

Color-changing LEDs and dimming functionality are powerful features that enhance the ambiance of your smart home. With RGB (Red, Green, Blue) LEDs or smart bulbs, you can change the color of the light and adjust brightness levels to match your preferences or the time of day.

Components Needed:

- **RGB LED Strip** (or smart bulb with RGB capabilities)
- **MOSFET or Transistor** (for controlling the LED strip)
- **Raspberry Pi**
- **Power Supply** (appropriate for the LED strip)

Using an RGB LED Strip with Raspberry Pi

1. **Connect the RGB LED Strip**:
   - Connect the **red, green, and blue pins** of the RGB LED strip to different **GPIO pins** on the Raspberry Pi.
   - Use **PWM (Pulse Width Modulation)** to control the brightness of each color channel.
2. **Controlling the RGB LED Strip**: Use Python's **RPi.GPIO** library and PWM to control the intensity of the red, green, and blue channels, thus changing the color of the light.

Python Script for Controlling RGB LED Strip

Here's a simple example of how to control the color of an RGB LED strip:

```python
```

```python
import RPi.GPIO as GPIO
import time

# Set GPIO mode and pins
GPIO.setmode(GPIO.BCM)
RED_PIN = 17
GREEN_PIN = 27
BLUE_PIN = 22
GPIO.setup(RED_PIN, GPIO.OUT)
GPIO.setup(GREEN_PIN, GPIO.OUT)
GPIO.setup(BLUE_PIN, GPIO.OUT)

# Set PWM frequency
red_pwm = GPIO.PWM(RED_PIN, 1000)
green_pwm = GPIO.PWM(GREEN_PIN, 1000)
blue_pwm = GPIO.PWM(BLUE_PIN, 1000)

# Start PWM
red_pwm.start(0)
green_pwm.start(0)
blue_pwm.start(0)

def set_color(r, g, b):
    red_pwm.ChangeDutyCycle(r)
    green_pwm.ChangeDutyCycle(g)
    blue_pwm.ChangeDutyCycle(b)

try:
    while True:
```

```
        set_color(100, 0, 0)   # Red
        time.sleep(1)
        set_color(0, 100, 0)   # Green
        time.sleep(1)
        set_color(0, 0, 100)   # Blue
        time.sleep(1)
        set_color(0, 0, 0)     # Off
        time.sleep(1)
except KeyboardInterrupt:
    GPIO.cleanup()   # Clean up GPIO on exit
```

This script uses PWM to control the color intensity of the RGB LED, cycling through red, green, blue, and off states. You can modify it to create dynamic lighting effects or match the color to a specific mood or time of day.

Integration with Voice Assistants (Google Assistant, Alexa)

Integrating your smart lighting system with voice assistants like **Google Assistant** or **Amazon Alexa** allows you to control the lights with simple voice commands. This adds a layer of convenience and accessibility to your smart home setup.

Integration with Google Assistant

To integrate Google Assistant with your Raspberry Pi and control lights, you will need to use the **Google Assistant SDK**.

1. **Install Google Assistant SDK**:
   o You can follow the official Google Assistant SDK documentation to install the necessary libraries and set up the voice assistant on your Raspberry Pi.
   o This typically involves setting up **OAuth** credentials and configuring the Assistant to recognize your Raspberry Pi as a device.

2. **Control Lights with Voice Commands**:
   o After setting up the Google Assistant SDK, you can configure it to control smart bulbs or other devices that you have connected to your Raspberry Pi. Commands like "Hey Google, turn on the lights" or "Hey Google, change the light color to blue" can trigger actions in your system.

Integration with Alexa

To integrate Alexa with your smart lighting system, you can use **Alexa Skills Kit** or **Alexa Smart Home API** to create a custom skill that can control the lights.

1. **Set Up Alexa Skills Kit**:
   - ○ You'll need to create an Alexa skill that can interface with your Raspberry Pi. This can be done by using **AWS Lambda** and setting up an endpoint on your Raspberry Pi that responds to Alexa commands.
   - ○ Follow Amazon's Alexa Smart Home documentation to create a custom skill and link it with your Raspberry Pi.

2. **Control Lights with Voice Commands**:
   - ○ Once the skill is set up, you can use commands like "Alexa, turn on the living room lights" or "Alexa, dim the bedroom lights to 50%" to control your automated lighting system.

Conclusion

Automating lighting with IoT sensors and Raspberry Pi can significantly improve the functionality, energy efficiency, and ambiance of your home. By using motion sensors to control lights based on occupancy, adding color-changing LEDs for customizable lighting, and integrating with voice assistants like Google Assistant and Alexa, you can create a truly intelligent and responsive lighting system. Whether for convenience, energy savings, or mood lighting, this chapter provides the tools to set up and expand your smart lighting system in a smart home.

CHAPTER 12

CREATING A SMART THERMOSTAT

A smart thermostat is a cornerstone of energy-efficient home automation. By using temperature sensors and integrating with other smart home devices, you can control your home's heating and cooling systems to maintain a comfortable environment while minimizing energy consumption. In this chapter, we will guide you through the process of building a smart thermostat using temperature sensors, adjusting heating and cooling systems based on room temperature, and integrating it with other home automation devices for added functionality.

How to Use Temperature Sensors to Build a Smart Thermostat

A smart thermostat works by constantly monitoring the room's temperature using sensors and adjusting the heating or cooling systems accordingly. Using Raspberry Pi and a temperature sensor like the **DHT22** or **LM35**, you can create a basic but effective thermostat.

119

Components Needed:

- **Raspberry Pi** (any model)
- **DHT22 Temperature and Humidity Sensor** (or LM35, or another temperature sensor)
- **Relay Module** (for controlling the heating/cooling system)
- **Smart Thermostat Application** (Python script or software interface)
- **Heating/Cooling Device** (such as a smart AC or heater, or a regular system controlled via relay)
- **Power Supply** (for Raspberry Pi and connected devices)

Wiring the Temperature Sensor to the Raspberry Pi

1. **Connect the DHT22 Sensor:**
   - **VCC** pin of the DHT22 sensor to the 5V pin on the Raspberry Pi.
   - **GND** pin to a GND pin on the Raspberry Pi.
   - **Data Pin** to a GPIO pin (e.g., GPIO 17). Make sure to include a **4.7kΩ resistor** between the data pin and the VCC pin to stabilize the signal.

2. **Connect the Relay to Raspberry Pi:**
   - **VCC** pin of the relay to the 5V pin on the Raspberry Pi.
   - **GND** pin to a GND pin on the Raspberry Pi.

- o **IN** pin of the relay to another GPIO pin (e.g., GPIO 18) to control the heating or cooling system.

3. **Connect the Heating/Cooling Device**:
   - o The relay will control the power to your heating or cooling system. For example, it could be connected to a smart heater or an air conditioning unit via a smart plug or directly if you're controlling a regular system with the relay.

Python Script for Monitoring Temperature and Controlling the Heating/Cooling System

Here's a Python script that reads temperature data from the DHT22 sensor and adjusts the heating or cooling system based on the room temperature.

```python
import Adafruit_DHT
import RPi.GPIO as GPIO
import time

# Set up GPIO pins
GPIO.setmode(GPIO.BCM)
RELAY_PIN = 18  # Relay pin for controlling heater
or AC
GPIO.setup(RELAY_PIN, GPIO.OUT)
```

121

```python
# Set the temperature threshold for heating and
cooling
min_temp = 20   # Temperature (C) to turn on
heating
max_temp = 25   # Temperature (C) to turn on
cooling

# Set up DHT22 sensor
sensor = Adafruit_DHT.DHT22
pin = 17  # GPIO pin connected to DHT22 data pin

def read_temperature():
    humidity,             temperature           =
Adafruit_DHT.read_retry(sensor, pin)
    if temperature is not None:
        return temperature
    else:
        print("Failed to read temperature")
        return None

def control_thermostat(temp):
    if temp is None:
        return

    if temp < min_temp:
        print(f"Temperature is {temp}°C, turning
on heating system.")
```

```
        GPIO.output(RELAY_PIN,   GPIO.HIGH)     #
Turn on heating
    elif temp > max_temp:
        print(f"Temperature is {temp}°C, turning
on cooling system.")
        GPIO.output(RELAY_PIN, GPIO.LOW)   # Turn
on cooling (or turn off heating)
    else:
        print(f"Temperature   is   {temp}°C,   no
action needed.")
        GPIO.output(RELAY_PIN,   GPIO.LOW)     #
Ensure system is off

try:
    while True:
        current_temp = read_temperature()
        print(f"Current            Temperature:
{current_temp}°C")
        control_thermostat(current_temp)
        time.sleep(60)  # Check every minute
except KeyboardInterrupt:
    GPIO.cleanup()  # Clean up GPIO on exit
```

Explanation:

- The **DHT22 sensor** reads the temperature, and the script compares it to the min_temp and max_temp thresholds.
- If the temperature falls below min_temp, the relay turns on the heating system.

- If the temperature exceeds `max_temp`, the relay controls the cooling system.
- If the temperature is within the ideal range, no action is taken.

Adjusting Heating and Cooling Systems Based on Room Temperature

Your smart thermostat will automatically adjust the heating and cooling systems based on the room temperature. Here's how it works in practice:

1. **Heating Control**: When the temperature falls below the minimum threshold (e.g., 20°C), the thermostat will activate the heating system, ensuring the room warms up.

2. **Cooling Control**: When the temperature rises above the maximum threshold (e.g., 25°C), the thermostat will activate the cooling system (e.g., air conditioning), ensuring the room cools down.

3. **Maintaining Comfort**: The thermostat ensures that the room stays within an ideal temperature range, avoiding unnecessary heating or cooling when the room temperature is already at a comfortable level.

Energy-Saving Considerations

Using a smart thermostat can save energy by reducing the heating or cooling when it's not needed. For example:

- If you set the temperature range to keep the room between 21°C and 23°C, your heating and cooling systems won't run all the time.
- You can also integrate occupancy sensors (such as PIR motion sensors) to turn off heating or cooling when the room is unoccupied, further saving energy.

Integrating with Other Home Automation Devices

Your smart thermostat can be even more powerful when integrated with other home automation devices. Below are a few ways to integrate it with the rest of your smart home system.

1. Integration with Smart Sensors and Devices

You can enhance the functionality of your smart thermostat by integrating it with additional sensors and devices in your home:

- **Occupancy Sensors**: Use a **PIR motion sensor** to detect when the room is unoccupied. If no one is in the room for

125

a set period, the thermostat can be programmed to turn off the heating or cooling system to save energy.

- **Light Sensors**: Integrate a light sensor to automatically adjust the temperature based on the time of day. For instance, if natural light is sufficient to warm the room, the thermostat could turn off the heating system.

2. Integration with Google Assistant or Alexa

By integrating your smart thermostat with **voice assistants**, you can control your home's temperature using voice commands. For example:

- **Google Assistant**: "Hey Google, set the living room temperature to 22°C."
- **Alexa**: "Alexa, increase the temperature by 2 degrees."

To integrate with Google Assistant or Alexa, you'll need to use platforms like **IFTTT** (If This Then That) or **Home Assistant**. These platforms can bridge your Raspberry Pi with Google or Amazon services, enabling voice control.

3. Integration with Smart Plugs

If you're using a regular heater or AC unit, you can integrate your smart thermostat with **smart plugs** to control the power supply to these devices. A smart plug can act as an on/off switch for non-smart heating and cooling systems.

- **Smart Plug Setup**: Plug your heater or air conditioner into a **Wi-Fi-enabled smart plug**, and use your Raspberry Pi to turn the plug on or off based on the temperature readings.

4. Integration with Home Assistant or OpenHAB

Home Assistant and **OpenHAB** are open-source platforms that allow you to integrate multiple smart devices into one central hub. By connecting your smart thermostat to these platforms, you can control the temperature from a unified interface and automate interactions with other devices (e.g., adjust the thermostat when lights are turned on).

For example, you could create an automation rule in Home Assistant: "When the lights turn off and no motion is detected for 30 minutes, set the thermostat to 18°C."

Conclusion

Building a smart thermostat using temperature sensors and Raspberry Pi is a great way to improve comfort and energy efficiency in your home. By adjusting heating and cooling systems based on real-time temperature data, you can ensure your home is always at the perfect temperature without wasting energy. Integrating with other IoT devices, such as motion sensors, smart plugs, and voice assistants, takes your thermostat to the next level, creating a fully automated home.

CHAPTER 13

VOICE CONTROL INTEGRATION

Voice control integration adds an extra layer of convenience and functionality to your smart home. With voice assistants like Google Assistant and Amazon Alexa, you can control your smart devices using simple voice commands, making it easier to interact with your home automation system. In this chapter, we will explore how to add voice assistants to your smart home, use APIs to control your Raspberry Pi and connected devices, and set up voice commands for common home automation tasks.

Adding Voice Assistants (Like Google Assistant or Amazon Alexa) to Your Smart Home

Voice assistants like **Google Assistant** and **Amazon Alexa** provide a seamless way to control various smart devices in your home, including lights, thermostats, security systems, and more. Integrating these assistants into your home automation system allows you to interact with your devices hands-free.

1. Setting Up Google Assistant with Raspberry Pi

To add Google Assistant to your Raspberry Pi, you need to set up the **Google Assistant SDK**. This SDK allows your Raspberry Pi to respond to voice commands and control connected devices.

Steps to Set Up Google Assistant on Raspberry Pi:

1. **Install Dependencies**: Begin by installing the required dependencies on your Raspberry Pi:

bash

```
sudo apt update
sudo apt install python3-dev python3-venv
sudo apt install libatlas-base-dev
sudo apt install portaudio19-dev
```

2. **Set Up Google Cloud Platform (GCP) and OAuth**:
   - Go to the **Google Cloud Console**: Google Cloud Console
   - Create a new project and enable the **Google Assistant API**.
   - Download your **OAuth 2.0 credentials** in the form of a `.json` file. This will allow Google Assistant to communicate securely with your Raspberry Pi.

3. **Install the Google Assistant SDK**:

   o Install the **Google Assistant SDK** on your Raspberry Pi by following the instructions in the Google Assistant SDK documentation.

   o Run the following command to install the required libraries:

   ```bash
   python3 -m pip install --upgrade google-assistant-sdk[samples]
   ```

4. **Authenticate Google Assistant**:

   o Run the authentication command to link your Raspberry Pi with your Google account:

   ```bash
   google-assistant-library --client-secrets /path/to/your/client_secret.json --project-id your_project_id
   ```

   o This will authorize Google Assistant to run on your Raspberry Pi.

5. **Test Google Assistant**: You can now use Google Assistant on your Raspberry Pi. Test it by running:

131

```bash
google-assistant-demo
```

You should be able to speak commands such as "Hey Google, what's the weather?" or "Hey Google, turn off the lights."

2. Setting Up Amazon Alexa with Raspberry Pi

Amazon Alexa integration can be done using the **Alexa Voice Service (AVS)**. Alexa allows you to control smart devices through the **Alexa Skills Kit (ASK)** or **Alexa Smart Home API**.

Steps to Set Up Alexa on Raspberry Pi:

1. **Sign Up for AVS**:
   o Sign up for an Amazon developer account and set up an **Alexa Voice Service** project on the Amazon Developer Console.
   o Download the **AVS SDK** and follow the instructions for setting up Alexa on a Raspberry Pi.
2. **Install Dependencies**: Run the following command to install the dependencies:

```bash
sudo apt-get update
sudo apt-get install git cmake build-essential
```

3. **Clone the AVS SDK**: Clone the AVS SDK repository and build it:

```bash
git clone https://github.com/alexa/avs-device-sdk.git
cd avs-device-sdk
mkdir build
cd build
cmake ..
make
```

4. **Authentication**:
   o Use **Alexa Voice Service** credentials to authenticate your Raspberry Pi as an Alexa-enabled device. Follow the AVS SDK documentation for detailed steps on creating an **Alexa Smart Home Skill** and linking the device to your Alexa account.

5. **Test Alexa**: After setting up, you can test voice commands by speaking to the Raspberry Pi: "Alexa,

turn on the living room lights" or "Alexa, play music."

Using APIs to Control Raspberry Pi and Connected Devices

Both Google Assistant and Amazon Alexa provide APIs that allow you to integrate your voice assistants with connected devices. These APIs enable you to control your Raspberry Pi, smart lights, thermostats, cameras, and other devices.

1. Using Google Assistant API to Control Raspberry Pi Devices

The **Google Assistant SDK** exposes an API that you can use to control Raspberry Pi devices. You can use **Google Cloud IoT**, **MQTT**, or **Home Assistant** for more advanced integrations.

Example of Controlling a GPIO Pin with Google Assistant:

Let's say you want to control a **light** connected to a Raspberry Pi using Google Assistant.

1. **Set Up MQTT on Raspberry Pi**: Install **MQTT** on your Raspberry Pi to communicate with Google Assistant.

```bash
sudo apt install mosquitto mosquitto-clients
```

2. **Control the Light via MQTT**: Create a Python script that listens for MQTT commands and controls the GPIO pin based on voice commands from Google Assistant.

```python
import paho.mqtt.client as mqtt
import RPi.GPIO as GPIO

# Set up GPIO
GPIO.setmode(GPIO.BCM)
GPIO.setup(18, GPIO.OUT)    # GPIO pin
connected to the relay or light

# MQTT callbacks
def on_connect(client, userdata, flags, rc):
    print(f"Connected to MQTT broker with result code {rc}")
    client.subscribe("home/lighting")

def on_message(client, userdata, msg):
    if msg.payload.decode() == "ON":
```

135

```
        GPIO.output(18, GPIO.HIGH)  # Turn
on light
    elif msg.payload.decode() == "OFF":
        GPIO.output(18, GPIO.LOW)   # Turn
off light

# MQTT client setup
client = mqtt.Client()
client.on_connect = on_connect
client.on_message = on_message
client.connect("mqtt.eclipse.org",   1883,
60)

client.loop_forever()
```

3. **Link Google Assistant with MQTT**: Use Google Assistant to publish messages to the MQTT broker (e.g., "turn on the light"). You can use **IFTTT** (If This Then That) to link Google Assistant to MQTT commands.

2. Using Alexa Smart Home API

The **Alexa Smart Home API** allows you to control your Raspberry Pi and connected devices via Alexa commands.

Example of Controlling a Raspberry Pi LED with Alexa:

1. **Set Up an Alexa Smart Home Skill**:
   - Go to the **Amazon Developer Console** and create a new **Smart Home Skill**.
   - Link the skill to your Raspberry Pi, and use the **Alexa Smart Home API** to receive commands like "Alexa, turn on the LED."

2. **Python Script for Controlling GPIO with Alexa**: You can control an LED connected to your Raspberry Pi by using the **Alexa Smart Home API** to trigger the GPIO pin:

```python
import RPi.GPIO as GPIO
import time

GPIO.setmode(GPIO.BCM)
GPIO.setup(17, GPIO.OUT)   # GPIO pin
connected to LED

while True:
    GPIO.output(17, GPIO.HIGH)   # Turn on
LED
    time.sleep(1)
    GPIO.output(17, GPIO.LOW)    # Turn off
LED
```

```
time.sleep(1)
```

Voice Commands for Common Home Automation Tasks

Once your voice assistants are integrated with Raspberry Pi and other devices, you can start using voice commands to control various tasks around your home. Below are some common examples of voice commands:

1. **Lighting Control**:
    o "Hey Google, turn on the kitchen lights."
    o "Alexa, set the living room lights to 50% brightness."
    o "Alexa, change the bedroom lights to blue."
2. **Temperature Control**:
    o "Hey Google, set the thermostat to 22°C."
    o "Alexa, increase the temperature in the living room by 2 degrees."
3. **Security System Control**:
    o "Hey Google, arm the security system."
    o "Alexa, show the front door camera."
4. **Media Control**:
    o "Alexa, play some music in the living room."
    o "Hey Google, pause the movie."
5. **Automation Triggers**:

o "Alexa, when I leave for work, turn off the lights and adjust the thermostat."

o "Hey Google, when motion is detected in the hallway, turn on the light."

Conclusion

Integrating voice control into your smart home with Google Assistant or Amazon Alexa adds an intuitive, hands-free way to interact with your home automation system. By using APIs to control Raspberry Pi and connected devices, you can create seamless automation and control various tasks using simple voice commands. Whether it's controlling lights, adjusting temperature, or activating security systems, voice assistants provide a convenient and modern way to manage your home.

CHAPTER 14

HOME AUTOMATION WITH CLOUD INTEGRATION

Cloud integration in home automation opens up new possibilities for managing and controlling your smart devices remotely, storing data securely, and automating tasks based on cloud-based intelligence. This chapter will introduce cloud platforms like **AWS (Amazon Web Services)**, **Google Cloud**, and others, and explain how you can use them for IoT in home automation. We will also cover how to store data in the cloud, access it remotely, and explore real-world examples of cloud-based smart home applications.

Introduction to Cloud Platforms (AWS, Google Cloud, etc.) for IoT

Cloud platforms such as **AWS**, **Google Cloud**, and **Microsoft Azure** offer powerful tools and services to connect IoT devices and facilitate automation, data storage, and remote control. These cloud platforms provide scalable infrastructure that allows you to manage large numbers of devices and perform advanced operations like data analysis and machine learning without needing to invest in expensive local hardware.

1. AWS IoT Core

AWS IoT Core is a managed cloud platform that enables you to connect Internet of Things (IoT) devices to the cloud. It facilitates the secure transfer of data between devices and cloud applications, allowing for remote control and automation.

Key features of AWS IoT Core:

- **Device Connectivity**: Allows devices to securely connect to the cloud using MQTT, HTTP, or WebSockets.
- **Security**: Built-in encryption and authentication mechanisms to ensure data security.
- **Data Processing**: AWS IoT Core integrates with other AWS services, such as AWS Lambda and Amazon S3, for processing and storing data.
- **Device Management**: Easily manage connected devices, monitor their health, and push updates.

2. Google Cloud IoT

Google Cloud IoT offers a suite of services for connecting, managing, and analyzing IoT data. It integrates with Google Cloud's data analytics and machine learning services, making it ideal for advanced IoT applications.

Key features of Google Cloud IoT:

- **Cloud IoT Core**: A fully managed service for securely connecting and managing IoT devices.
- **Data Analysis**: Google Cloud integrates with BigQuery and Google Cloud's AI services for advanced data analysis and real-time insights.
- **Security**: Google Cloud provides end-to-end encryption and authentication.
- **Edge Computing**: With **Cloud IoT Edge**, you can perform data processing at the edge (on the device) for faster responses and reduced latency.

3. Microsoft Azure IoT

Microsoft Azure IoT offers a range of tools to help connect, monitor, and manage IoT devices. Azure IoT Hub is the central service for connecting devices, while other services like **Azure Stream Analytics** and **Azure Machine Learning** provide advanced data processing and analytics.

142

Key features of Microsoft Azure IoT:

- **IoT Hub**: Securely connects and manages IoT devices, enabling two-way communication between devices and the cloud.
- **Azure Machine Learning**: Leverages AI to analyze data from IoT devices and make intelligent predictions or automated decisions.
- **Device Management**: Provides monitoring, diagnostics, and provisioning capabilities for connected devices.

Storing Data in the Cloud and Accessing It Remotely

One of the primary advantages of cloud integration is the ability to store data from IoT devices securely in the cloud, which can then be accessed remotely. This enables users to monitor and control devices from anywhere, regardless of their physical location.

1. Storing Data in the Cloud

Cloud storage solutions are ideal for storing large amounts of data generated by IoT devices. Cloud platforms offer multiple options for data storage:

- **AWS S3 (Simple Storage Service)**: Amazon's scalable object storage service is ideal for storing large amounts of unstructured data, such as images, videos, or sensor data.

- **Google Cloud Storage**: Google's object storage service is optimized for high availability and scalability, making it perfect for storing IoT data.

- **Microsoft Azure Blob Storage**: Azure provides highly scalable object storage for unstructured data, which is ideal for storing data from IoT sensors.

2. Accessing Data Remotely

Once the data is stored in the cloud, it can be accessed remotely via APIs, web interfaces, or mobile applications. For example:

- **Mobile Apps**: You can build mobile apps that allow users to view live data from IoT devices or check historical data stored in the cloud.

- **Web Dashboards**: Create a web-based dashboard to monitor and control devices in real-time. For example, a smart thermostat's temperature readings can be shown on a dashboard.

- **APIs**: Cloud platforms provide RESTful APIs that allow applications to retrieve, update, or process data remotely. This is especially useful for integrating cloud-based data with other home automation systems.

For example, you can use AWS API Gateway or Google Cloud Functions to create APIs that allow your smartphone or another device to retrieve the current temperature from a smart thermostat, regardless of where you are.

3. Data Security and Backup

Cloud platforms also offer built-in security and backup solutions to ensure that your data is safe and can be recovered if needed:

- **Encryption**: Data can be encrypted both in transit and at rest using encryption protocols such as SSL/TLS for transport and AES-256 for storage.
- **Backups**: Cloud providers offer automated backup services, ensuring that data is preserved and can be restored in case of failure.

Real-World Examples of Cloud-Based Smart Home Applications

Cloud integration brings immense possibilities to smart home applications. Below are a few real-world examples of how cloud-based IoT solutions are being used for home automation.

1. Smart Thermostats (e.g., Nest Thermostat)

Smart thermostats, like the **Nest Thermostat**, use cloud-based platforms to monitor temperature, learn user preferences, and control heating or cooling systems. Data from temperature sensors in the home is sent to the cloud, where machine learning algorithms analyze usage patterns. The thermostat can then adjust the home's temperature automatically, ensuring energy efficiency while maintaining comfort.

Cloud Integration: The thermostat's data is sent to Google Cloud, where it is processed and used to provide remote access via the **Google Home** app. Users can control the thermostat remotely from anywhere, set schedules, and receive notifications if the temperature goes outside the set range.

2. Smart Lighting (e.g., Philips Hue)

Smart lighting systems like **Philips Hue** allow users to control their lights remotely, set schedules, and change colors using a cloud-based platform. Data about light usage, user preferences, and energy consumption is stored in the cloud and accessible via mobile apps or voice commands.

Cloud Integration: Philips Hue integrates with platforms like **Google Assistant** and **Amazon Alexa** via cloud APIs. The data is stored in the cloud, allowing users to remotely control their lights and automate lighting based on their routines or external factors such as time of day or occupancy.

3. Home Security Systems (e.g., Ring Video Doorbell)

Smart home security systems, like **Ring Video Doorbell**, use cameras and sensors to monitor activity at the front door. Video footage is stored in the cloud, making it accessible from any device, even if the camera is stolen or damaged.

Cloud Integration: Ring integrates with AWS for storing video footage in the cloud. It uses AWS IoT services to communicate with the devices and **AWS S3** for storing recorded video. Users can access live and recorded footage remotely through the **Ring mobile app**.

4. Energy Management (e.g., EnergyHub)

Energy management systems, like **EnergyHub**, provide real-time monitoring of energy usage in a home and allow users to automate energy-saving tasks, such as turning off appliances when they are not in use or adjusting thermostats for efficiency.

Cloud Integration: EnergyHub uses cloud-based platforms like **Google Cloud** to aggregate data from various smart devices, including thermostats, lights, and energy meters. The platform allows users to view their energy usage trends, receive notifications, and control their devices remotely.

Conclusion

Cloud integration is essential for modern home automation, enabling remote control, data storage, and advanced processing of IoT data. Platforms like **AWS**, **Google Cloud**, and **Microsoft Azure** provide powerful tools to manage and control IoT devices in real-time. By leveraging these cloud services, you can create scalable, secure, and efficient smart home systems that provide convenience, energy savings, and automation. Real-world examples, such as smart thermostats, lighting, security systems, and energy management platforms, demonstrate how cloud-based solutions are transforming the way we interact with our homes.

CHAPTER 15

SMART IRRIGATION SYSTEMS

Watering plants efficiently is essential for both conserving resources and maintaining healthy plants. Traditional irrigation systems often waste water due to over-watering or irregular schedules. By using **IoT-based smart irrigation systems**, you can automate watering based on real-time soil moisture data, ensuring that plants receive just the right amount of water. In this chapter, we will guide you through using **soil moisture sensors** to automate irrigation, designing a water-efficient smart garden system, and integrating **Raspberry Pi** to control irrigation schedules.

How to Use Soil Moisture Sensors for Automated Irrigation

Soil moisture sensors are devices that measure the water content in the soil. By integrating these sensors with a microcontroller like Raspberry Pi, you can automate irrigation systems that activate watering based on soil moisture levels, preventing over-watering and ensuring plants receive the optimal amount of water.

Components Needed:

- **Soil Moisture Sensor** (e.g., capacitive or resistive type)
- **Raspberry Pi** (any model with GPIO pins)
- **Relay Module** (to control the irrigation valve or pump)
- **Water Pump or Solenoid Valve** (for irrigation)
- **Tubing or Watering System** (for distributing water to the plants)
- **Power Supply** (for Raspberry Pi and connected devices)
- **Jumper Wires** (for connecting the components)

Wiring the Soil Moisture Sensor and Irrigation System

1. **Soil Moisture Sensor**:
   - Connect the **VCC** pin of the soil moisture sensor to the **5V pin** on the Raspberry Pi.
   - Connect the **GND** pin of the sensor to a **GND pin** on the Raspberry Pi.
   - Connect the **A0 (Analog)** or **D0 (Digital)** pin (depending on your sensor) to a **GPIO pin** on the Raspberry Pi (e.g., GPIO 17 for analog, GPIO 18 for digital).

2. **Relay Module**:
   - Connect the **VCC** pin of the relay module to the **5V** pin on the Raspberry Pi.
   - Connect the **GND** pin to the **GND** pin on the Raspberry Pi.

150

- Connect the **IN** pin of the relay to another GPIO pin (e.g., GPIO 23).
- Connect the relay's **NO (Normally Open)** and **COM (Common)** pins to the water pump or irrigation solenoid valve to control water flow.

Python Script for Automating Irrigation Based on Soil Moisture

The goal of this script is to read data from the soil moisture sensor and activate the irrigation system when the soil moisture level falls below a set threshold.

```python
import RPi.GPIO as GPIO
import time

# Set GPIO mode
GPIO.setmode(GPIO.BCM)

# Define GPIO pins for soil moisture sensor and
relay
MOISTURE_PIN = 17  # GPIO pin for soil moisture
sensor
RELAY_PIN = 23  # GPIO pin for relay control

# Set up GPIO pins
GPIO.setup(MOISTURE_PIN, GPIO.IN)
GPIO.setup(RELAY_PIN, GPIO.OUT)
```

151

```python
# Define moisture threshold (adjust based on
sensor calibration)
MOISTURE_THRESHOLD = 500  # Example threshold for
dry soil


# Function to check soil moisture level
def read_soil_moisture():
    moisture_level = GPIO.input(MOISTURE_PIN)  #
Read moisture level
    return moisture_level


# Function to control irrigation system
def control_irrigation(moisture_level):
    if moisture_level < MOISTURE_THRESHOLD:
        print("Soil     is     dry.     Starting
irrigation...")
        GPIO.output(RELAY_PIN,   GPIO.HIGH)     #
Turn on irrigation
    else:
        print("Soil    is    sufficiently    moist.
Stopping irrigation...")
        GPIO.output(RELAY_PIN, GPIO.LOW)  # Turn
off irrigation


# Main loop
try:
    while True:
```

```
        soil_moisture = read_soil_moisture()   #
Get moisture level
        print(f"Soil        moisture        level:
{soil_moisture}")
        control_irrigation(soil_moisture)      #
Control irrigation based on moisture
        time.sleep(10)   # Check every 10 seconds

except KeyboardInterrupt:
    GPIO.cleanup()   # Clean up GPIO on exit
```

Explanation:

- The **soil moisture sensor** provides data that is either analog or digital. For simplicity, we assume a digital sensor in this example.

- If the **soil moisture level** falls below the predefined threshold (MOISTURE_THRESHOLD), the system activates the irrigation system by turning on the relay.

- The relay controls a **water pump** or **solenoid valve**, which then waters the plants. If the soil is sufficiently moist, the system will turn off the irrigation.

Designing a Water-Efficient Smart Garden System

One of the key benefits of a smart irrigation system is that it ensures **efficient water usage** by only watering plants when necessary. Designing a water-efficient garden involves not only automating irrigation but also optimizing it to minimize water waste.

1. Selecting the Right Sensors and Irrigation System

To maximize water efficiency, consider the following when setting up your smart garden system:

- **Soil Moisture Sensors**: Use **capacitive soil moisture sensors** instead of resistive ones, as they provide more accurate readings and are less affected by corrosion.
- **Drip Irrigation**: Instead of using traditional sprinklers, consider using **drip irrigation**, which delivers water directly to the plant roots, minimizing evaporation and runoff.
- **Multiple Zones**: Divide your garden into multiple zones with separate moisture sensors. This allows you to water different parts of your garden according to their specific needs. For example, the vegetable garden may need more frequent watering than flower beds.

2. Creating Watering Schedules

You can integrate your smart irrigation system with a **scheduler** to water plants at optimal times. For example:

- **Time of Day**: Set the system to water in the early morning or late evening when evaporation is minimal.

- **Weather Data Integration**: Use cloud services like **Google Cloud** or **AWS IoT** to integrate weather data. If it's going to rain, the system can skip watering for the day.

- **Soil Type Considerations**: Different plants and soil types have different water retention rates. By grouping plants with similar needs into different irrigation zones, you can optimize watering schedules.

3. Monitoring Water Usage

Using cloud integration, you can store and monitor your garden's water usage over time. For example:

- **Data Logging**: Record irrigation events, water usage, and soil moisture levels in the cloud. This data can help you adjust watering schedules and make your system even more efficient.

- **Remote Monitoring**: Access your garden's status remotely through a smartphone app or web interface. You can see the moisture levels in real-time and even manually override the system if necessary.

Integrating Raspberry Pi to Control Irrigation Schedules

Raspberry Pi can serve as the central controller for your automated irrigation system, enabling more complex scheduling and integration with other devices.

1. Using a Real-Time Clock (RTC) for Schedules

If you want your irrigation system to water at specific times of day (e.g., early morning or late evening), you can use an **RTC module** with Raspberry Pi to schedule irrigation.

Example:

You can use Python's `time` module to check the time and activate the irrigation system at set intervals:

```python
import time
import RPi.GPIO as GPIO
from datetime import datetime

# Set up GPIO for relay (as in previous examples)
GPIO.setmode(GPIO.BCM)
RELAY_PIN = 23
GPIO.setup(RELAY_PIN, GPIO.OUT)

# Define the time of day to activate watering
(e.g., 6 AM)
```

156

```
WATERING_TIME = "06:00:00"

# Main loop
try:
    while True:
        current_time                          =
datetime.now().strftime("%H:%M:%S")
        if current_time == WATERING_TIME:
            print("It's watering time!")
            GPIO.output(RELAY_PIN, GPIO.HIGH)  #
Activate watering
        else:
            GPIO.output(RELAY_PIN, GPIO.LOW)   #
Turn off watering
        time.sleep(60)   # Check every minute

except KeyboardInterrupt:
    GPIO.cleanup()  # Clean up GPIO on exit
```

This script activates the irrigation system at the specified time (6 AM in this case) and checks every minute if it's time to water.

2. Cloud Integration for Remote Control and Monitoring

By integrating your Raspberry Pi irrigation system with cloud services like **AWS IoT**, **Google Cloud**, or **Home Assistant**, you can remotely monitor and control your irrigation system. For example, you could set up an API to turn the irrigation system on or off from anywhere using a mobile app.

You can also store data on cloud platforms for long-term analysis, such as tracking moisture levels, water consumption, and irrigation schedules, which helps optimize water usage over time.

Conclusion

Creating a smart irrigation system with Raspberry Pi and soil moisture sensors is an effective way to automate garden watering, conserve water, and maintain healthy plants. By integrating sensors, scheduling, and cloud-based services, you can ensure that your garden receives just the right amount of water at the right time. This water-efficient system not only reduces water waste but also makes managing your garden more convenient and accessible from anywhere.

CHAPTER 16

BUILDING A HOME AUTOMATION DASHBOARD

A home automation dashboard is an essential tool for controlling and monitoring the various smart devices in your home. It acts as the central hub where you can view sensor data, control devices, and automate tasks. In this chapter, we will explore how to use software like **Node-RED** to create a control dashboard for your smart home. We will also cover how to visualize sensor data and control devices from a single interface and discuss the basics of designing a web interface for smart home control.

Using Node-RED or Other Software for Creating a Control Dashboard

Node-RED is a flow-based programming tool that allows you to wire together devices, APIs, and online services for home automation. It's an ideal platform for creating a home automation dashboard because of its ease of use and flexibility.

1. What is Node-RED?

Node-RED is an open-source tool built on Node.js that provides a visual interface for wiring together hardware devices and services. It allows you to design workflows that control your smart home devices using a drag-and-drop interface. Node-RED can integrate with various IoT protocols such as MQTT, HTTP, and WebSockets, making it an excellent tool for building a smart home control dashboard.

2. Installing Node-RED on Raspberry Pi

To get started, you'll need to install Node-RED on your Raspberry Pi. Follow these steps:

1. Open the terminal on your Raspberry Pi.
2. Run the following command to install Node-RED:

```bash
bash

bash             <(curl           -sL
https://raw.githubusercontent.com/node-
red/linux-installers/master/deb/setup.sh)
```

3. Once installation is complete, start Node-RED by typing:

```
bash
```

```
node-red-start
```

4. Open a web browser and navigate to `http://<your-pi-ip>:1880` to access the Node-RED dashboard interface.

3. Creating a Basic Dashboard in Node-RED

To create a home automation dashboard in Node-RED:

1. **Add Devices and Sensors**: Start by dragging and dropping nodes for your devices, sensors, or other inputs. For example, you can add a **temperature sensor node**, a **light control node**, and a **motion sensor node**.

2. **Define Actions and Outputs**: Define the actions that should happen when certain conditions are met. For example, when the temperature exceeds a certain value, turn on the air conditioner.

3. **Use the Dashboard Nodes**: Node-RED includes specific nodes for creating a user interface (UI) for your dashboard. To add these nodes:
    o   Drag the **UI nodes** (like **button**, **gauge**, **slider**, **chart**, and **text** nodes) to the flow.

161

o Link these nodes to the corresponding device control nodes. For example, you could link a **button node** that turns on a light or a **slider node** to control the brightness.

4. **Deploy the Dashboard**: Once the flows are designed, deploy your Node-RED project. The UI will be available at a URL (e.g., `http://<your-pi-ip>:1880/ui`). You can now access it from a web browser to control your devices and view real-time data.

Visualizing Sensor Data and Controlling Devices from a Central Interface

A central dashboard gives you a real-time overview of your home's smart devices and sensor data. This makes it easier to manage and automate your home. With Node-RED, you can visualize data from sensors and control devices directly from the dashboard.

1. Visualizing Sensor Data

To visualize sensor data, use **chart nodes** or **gauge nodes** in the Node-RED dashboard.

1. **Chart Node**: Displays real-time graphs of data, such as temperature, humidity, or energy usage.
   - o For example, you can add a chart that plots the temperature data from a DHT22 sensor over time.
2. **Gauge Node**: Displays a dial or a numeric representation of a value.
   - o For instance, a gauge could show the current temperature or the soil moisture level in your garden.
3. **Text Node**: Displays the current value of a sensor, such as the humidity or the light status.

2. Controlling Devices

You can use UI controls in Node-RED to interact with devices directly from your dashboard. Common controls include:

- **Button**: A simple on/off control to activate or deactivate a device.
- **Slider**: A control for adjusting values, such as the brightness of a light or the thermostat temperature.
- **Switch**: A toggle for turning a device on or off, such as activating a fan or switching a light on.

For example, to control a light:

1. Add a **button node** to the dashboard for controlling the light.
2. Connect the button to a **GPIO output node** (or a relay node if controlling a non-smart device).
3. When the button is clicked, the corresponding action (turning the light on or off) will happen.

Example Flow for Controlling a Light:

1. **Button Node**: Adds a button to the dashboard.
2. **GPIO Output Node**: Controls a relay or a smart bulb.
3. **Function Node**: Optional, for additional logic such as checking if a device is already on.

This flow ensures that you can easily control your devices with a simple user interface.

Web Interface Design Basics for Smart Home Control

Designing an effective web interface for controlling your smart home devices is essential for a smooth user experience. Here are some basic principles for creating a functional and intuitive dashboard:

1. User-Friendly Layout

- **Simplicity**: Avoid clutter and ensure that the layout is simple and intuitive. Group related devices (e.g., lights, temperature control, security system) together on different tabs or sections of the dashboard.
- **Responsive Design**: Make sure your interface is responsive, meaning it adjusts well to different screen sizes, from desktops to smartphones. This is particularly important if you want to control your smart home from a mobile device.
- **Clear Labels**: Clearly label each control (e.g., "Living Room Light", "Thermostat", "Security Camera") to ensure users understand what they are controlling.

2. Visual Feedback

- Use visual elements like **color changes** or **icons** to indicate the status of devices. For example, a green icon for an active light and a red icon for a turned-off light.
- Display **real-time data** from sensors, such as temperature, humidity, or motion detection, so users can see the current status at a glance.

3. Device Control

- Include **toggle switches**, **buttons**, or **sliders** to allow users to control devices (lights, temperature, cameras, etc.) directly from the interface.
- For advanced controls, such as thermostat settings, provide **sliders** or **input fields** to set specific values (e.g., set the temperature to 22°C).

4. Automated Actions

- Add **automation buttons** or toggle switches to enable or disable automated actions, like turning on lights when motion is detected or adjusting the thermostat based on the time of day.
- Allow users to set their preferences, such as the time of day when devices should be activated or deactivated (e.g., turning off lights at night or adjusting the heating during the evening).

5. Graphical Representation

- Use **charts** or **graphs** to display sensor data visually, such as the temperature history or motion events over the past 24 hours. This makes the data more accessible and easier to interpret.

Example Web Interface Design:

- **Dashboard Layout**:
    - **Top Bar**: Includes the current date, time, and quick access to the system settings.
    - **Main Section**: Divided into sections like "Lights," "Temperature," "Security," etc.
    - **Controls**: Sliders for lights, buttons for toggling devices, charts for sensor data.
- **Responsive Design**:
    - The dashboard layout automatically adjusts when viewed on a smartphone, ensuring the controls remain easy to use.

Conclusion

Building a home automation dashboard using Node-RED or other similar software is a powerful way to control and monitor your smart home. With real-time sensor data visualization, device control, and automated actions, your dashboard will allow for an intuitive and efficient smart home experience. By following web design best practices and focusing on a user-friendly layout, you can create an interface that provides both functionality and accessibility. Whether you're controlling lights, monitoring security, or adjusting temperature, a well-designed dashboard is key to managing your home automation system effectively.

CHAPTER 17

VOICE-ACTIVATED SMART APPLIANCES

Voice-activated smart appliances are revolutionizing the way we interact with our homes, providing convenience, efficiency, and accessibility. By integrating voice control with appliances such as smart fridges, ovens, washing machines, and even non-smart appliances, we can create a more seamless and automated living environment. In this chapter, we will explore how to integrate voice control with various appliances, use voice commands to control non-smart appliances, and connect appliances to **Raspberry Pi** and **IoT sensors** for smarter, more automated control.

Integration with Appliances such as Smart Fridges, Ovens, and Washing Machines

Smart appliances like fridges, ovens, and washing machines are already equipped with built-in connectivity, allowing them to integrate with home automation systems. By combining these appliances with **voice assistants** like

Amazon Alexa or **Google Assistant**, you can control them with simple voice commands.

1. Smart Fridge Integration

Smart fridges are equipped with Wi-Fi connectivity, sensors, and sometimes even touchscreens, allowing them to monitor and manage food inventory, control temperature settings, and offer real-time notifications.

Example Integration:

- **Voice Command**: "Alexa, what's the temperature of the fridge?" or "Google, check if we have eggs in the fridge."
- **How It Works**: The fridge sends temperature and inventory data to a cloud-based service, which then communicates with your voice assistant to provide responses.

You can also integrate a smart fridge with a **Raspberry Pi** to monitor and control temperature settings or track items in the fridge via sensors. For instance, using a **temperature sensor** connected to the Raspberry Pi, you can adjust cooling settings based on sensor readings or set alerts if the fridge temperature falls outside an optimal range.

2. Smart Oven Integration

Smart ovens allow you to control temperature settings, cooking modes, and timers remotely, as well as monitor the cooking process in real-time.

Example Integration:

- **Voice Command**: "Alexa, preheat the oven to 180°C," or "Google, set the oven timer for 30 minutes."
- **How It Works**: The oven is connected to the internet and communicates with your voice assistant through a cloud-based service. By enabling voice commands, you can control your oven with just your voice.

You can integrate a smart oven with **Raspberry Pi** to collect data like the internal temperature or cooking mode. This data can be visualized or logged, allowing you to set up custom notifications or automated cooking schedules.

3. Smart Washing Machine Integration

Smart washing machines enable remote control, monitoring, and scheduling of washing cycles. These appliances often have sensors to detect load size, water temperature, and detergent levels, allowing for more efficient washing.

Example Integration:

- **Voice Command**: "Alexa, start the washing machine," or "Google, how long is the laundry cycle?"
- **How It Works**: The washing machine connects to the cloud to communicate with your voice assistant, enabling control over the wash cycle, water temperature, and washing mode.

Through **Raspberry Pi** and IoT sensors, you can enhance your washing machine's capabilities by monitoring factors like water usage, cycle duration, and energy consumption. You could also trigger alerts when the cycle is complete or if the machine detects an issue, such as an unbalanced load.

Using Voice Commands to Control Non-Smart Appliances

While many modern appliances come with built-in voice assistant compatibility, you can also use voice control with non-smart appliances by connecting them to a **Raspberry Pi** and integrating smart plugs, relays, or sensors.

1. Non-Smart Appliances with Smart Plugs

If you have a non-smart appliance, such as a coffee maker, fan, or heater, you can convert it into a smart appliance by plugging it into a **smart plug**. Smart plugs are Wi-Fi-enabled outlets that allow you to control non-smart appliances via a smartphone app or voice assistant.

Example Setup:

- **Smart Plug Integration**: Plug your coffee maker or fan into a smart plug. Then connect the smart plug to a voice assistant like Alexa or Google Assistant.
- **Voice Command**: "Alexa, turn on the coffee maker," or "Google, turn off the fan."

2. Voice-Activated Control Using Raspberry Pi

For more advanced setups, you can connect non-smart appliances to a **Raspberry Pi** using **relays** and **GPIO pins**. By programming the Raspberry Pi and integrating it with a voice assistant, you can control any appliance that can be activated through a relay (e.g., a lamp, fan, or toaster).

Example Setup:

- **Relay Module**: Connect the relay module to the Raspberry Pi's GPIO pins and wire the appliance to the relay.
- **Voice Command Integration**: Use **Alexa Skills Kit (ASK)** or **Google Actions** to create custom voice commands that activate the relay through your Raspberry Pi. For example, a command like "Alexa, turn on the lamp" would trigger the relay to close the circuit and power the appliance.

Connecting Appliances to Raspberry Pi and IoT Sensors

To take your voice-controlled appliances to the next level, you can integrate **IoT sensors** with **Raspberry Pi** to gather data and automate actions based on specific conditions.

1. Temperature Sensors for Appliances

For appliances like fridges and ovens, **temperature sensors** (e.g., **DHT22** or **DS18B20**) can be connected to Raspberry Pi to monitor the internal temperature. This data can then be used for automation.

Example: Smart Fridge Monitoring

- **Sensor**: Attach a temperature sensor to monitor the fridge's temperature.
- **Automation**: Use Python to read the temperature data and send an alert to your phone or activate the refrigerator's cooling system if the temperature exceeds a set threshold.

2. Energy Monitoring for Non-Smart Appliances

By using **energy monitoring plugs** or **current sensors** (like the **INA219**), you can track energy usage for non-smart appliances. This data can be collected and visualized on a dashboard, or it can trigger automated actions based on energy consumption.

Example: Monitoring Appliance Energy Usage

- **Sensor**: Plug your washing machine into an energy monitoring plug.
- **Automation**: Track the energy usage and trigger notifications if the usage is too high or if the appliance runs for longer than expected.

3. Relay-Controlled Appliance Automation

Raspberry Pi can control **high-voltage appliances** via **relay modules**, making it a great tool for automating non-smart devices. By connecting a relay to the Raspberry Pi's GPIO pins, you can turn appliances on or off remotely.

Example: Controlling a Lamp

- **Relay Module**: Connect a relay to the Raspberry Pi and wire it to a lamp.
- **Automation**: Create a Node-RED flow or a Python script that uses a voice assistant to control the lamp, allowing you to turn it on or off with voice commands.

Example Python Code for Voice Control of Non-Smart Appliances via Raspberry Pi

Below is a simple Python example that shows how you can control an appliance through a relay using Raspberry Pi and a voice assistant. You can integrate this code with **Alexa** or **Google Assistant** using **IFTTT** or by creating custom skills.

```
python

import RPi.GPIO as GPIO
import time
```

```
# Set up GPIO pin
GPIO.setmode(GPIO.BCM)
RELAY_PIN = 18  # GPIO pin connected to relay
GPIO.setup(RELAY_PIN, GPIO.OUT)

# Function to control the appliance
def turn_on_appliance():
    GPIO.output(RELAY_PIN, GPIO.HIGH)  # Turn on
appliance
    print("Appliance turned ON")

def turn_off_appliance():
    GPIO.output(RELAY_PIN, GPIO.LOW)  # Turn off
appliance
    print("Appliance turned OFF")

# Main loop (For testing purpose)
try:
    while True:
        user_input = input("Enter 'on' to turn on
or 'off' to turn off the appliance: ")
        if user_input == "on":
            turn_on_appliance()
        elif user_input == "off":
            turn_off_appliance()
        else:
            print("Invalid input.")
except KeyboardInterrupt:
```

```
GPIO.cleanup()
```

This script will turn the appliance on or off based on user input. You can replace the input logic with voice control integration to activate the appliance using voice commands.

Conclusion

Voice-activated smart appliances make everyday tasks more convenient, and integrating them into your home automation system allows you to control and monitor devices hands-free. By using **voice assistants** like **Alexa** or **Google Assistant**, you can control both smart and non-smart appliances through simple voice commands. Integrating these appliances with **Raspberry Pi** and **IoT sensors** opens up even more possibilities for automation, monitoring, and energy efficiency. Whether you are controlling a smart oven or automating non-smart appliances using relays, voice control offers seamless integration and convenience for modern smart homes.

CHAPTER 18

INTEGRATING SMART LOCKS

Smart locks are a critical component of modern home automation, offering greater convenience, enhanced security, and the ability to remotely control door entry. They allow homeowners to lock and unlock doors using a smartphone, key fob, or even voice commands. In this chapter, we will cover how to set up **smart locks**, automate door entry, integrate them with other IoT devices like cameras and motion sensors, and explore the security and privacy concerns associated with using smart locks.

Setting Up Smart Locks and Automating Door Entry

Smart locks are designed to replace traditional mechanical locks with electronic ones that can be controlled remotely. The basic setup typically involves installing the smart lock on your door and connecting it to your home automation system via Wi-Fi, Bluetooth, or Zigbee.

1. Installing a Smart Lock

When installing a smart lock, follow these general steps:

- **Remove the old lock**: Unscrew and remove your existing deadbolt or doorknob.
- **Install the smart lock hardware**: Follow the instructions provided by the manufacturer to install the smart lock hardware. This typically involves fixing the locking mechanism and aligning it with the door frame.
- **Connect the lock to your home network**: Smart locks connect via Wi-Fi, Bluetooth, or Zigbee to a central hub or directly to a smartphone app. Make sure you connect the lock to the appropriate network and follow the pairing instructions.

2. Smart Lock Features

- **Remote Control**: Smart locks can be controlled from anywhere using a smartphone app. This means you can lock or unlock the door from your office, the car, or even while on vacation.
- **Keyless Entry**: Instead of using traditional keys, smart locks allow you to unlock your door via an app, a PIN code, or a Bluetooth connection.
- **Automated Entry**: Some smart locks support features like auto-locking and unlocking. For example, the lock

can automatically unlock as you approach the door with your phone (using Bluetooth or geofencing).

3. Automating Door Entry

Smart locks can be integrated with your home automation system to automate the locking and unlocking process. For example:

- **Auto-locking**: You can set the lock to automatically engage after a certain time or when the door is closed.
- **Remote Unlocking**: If you want to give someone access to your home, you can unlock the door remotely via an app or voice command.
- **Voice Control**: Integrate your smart lock with voice assistants like **Alexa** or **Google Assistant** to unlock the door via voice commands, such as "Alexa, unlock the front door."

Example integration with **Node-RED**:

- Create an automation that unlocks the door when motion is detected by a **PIR motion sensor** or when the time of day reaches a certain hour (e.g., unlocking the door at 6 PM every day).

Here is a basic example using **Node-RED**:

1. **Input**: Motion sensor detects a person.
2. **Output**: Smart lock is unlocked after the motion is detected, and a notification is sent.

Integration with Other IoT Devices (Cameras, Motion Sensors)

Integrating your smart lock with other IoT devices such as **cameras** and **motion sensors** increases the security of your home and provides more automation options. For example, you can set up your system to unlock the door when it detects a known person via a **security camera** or only unlock when the motion sensor confirms that the right person is at the door.

1. Integration with Security Cameras

Security cameras can work in tandem with smart locks to provide a layer of security and confirm who is at your door before unlocking it.

How it works:

- When someone presses the doorbell or approaches the door, the security camera detects motion.

- The camera sends a live feed or image to your smartphone, and you can view it via an app.
- If the visitor is recognized (e.g., through facial recognition or a live feed), you can unlock the door remotely.

You can integrate your camera with the smart lock by using **Home Assistant**, **IFTTT**, or **Node-RED** to link the two devices. For example, you could create an automation where:

- If the security camera detects a known face, the smart lock will unlock.
- If the motion sensor detects movement at night, the camera will start recording, and the door will remain locked.

2. Integration with Motion Sensors

Motion sensors can trigger events based on activity near the door, adding another layer of security and automation to your smart lock system. Motion sensors can detect when someone is at the door, and the smart lock can automatically unlock when the motion sensor confirms the presence of a person.

Example Setup:

- **Motion Sensor**: Detects someone approaching the door.
- **Smart Lock**: Unlocks once the motion sensor confirms the person's presence.
- **Security Camera**: Starts recording if the motion sensor is triggered.
- **Voice Assistant**: Notifies you about the motion detection or lets you see a live feed of the person at the door.

This integration provides more control over the security and convenience of accessing your home, especially when combined with facial recognition or other verification systems.

Security and Privacy Concerns When Using Smart Locks

While smart locks offer convenience, they also come with potential security and privacy risks. It is important to be aware of these risks and take necessary precautions.

1. Data Breaches and Hacking Risks

Since smart locks are connected to the internet, they can be vulnerable to hacking if not properly secured.

Cybercriminals can exploit weak security settings to gain access to your home remotely.

Mitigation Steps:

- **Use Strong Passwords**: Ensure your smart lock app and home network are protected by strong, unique passwords.
- **Enable Two-Factor Authentication (2FA)**: Many smart lock providers offer 2FA, which adds an extra layer of security when accessing the lock remotely.
- **Regular Updates**: Keep the firmware of your smart lock up to date to patch any known security vulnerabilities.
- **Use Encrypted Communication**: Choose smart locks that use encryption (e.g., AES or SSL) to protect communication between the device and the app.

2. Bluetooth and Wi-Fi Vulnerabilities

Bluetooth and Wi-Fi communication protocols can also be targets for hackers. For example, if a Bluetooth smart lock is not configured with secure pairing or has a weak encryption algorithm, it may be susceptible to attacks.

Mitigation Steps:

- **Use Secure Pairing**: When setting up your smart lock, ensure it uses secure Bluetooth pairing (e.g., BLE 5.0 with AES encryption).
- **Use Trusted Networks**: Ensure that your home Wi-Fi network is secured with WPA3 encryption and a strong password.
- **Avoid Using Default Settings**: Change the default PIN or codes for the smart lock and use a unique identification for each device.

3. Privacy Concerns with Cameras and Motion Sensors

Using smart locks alongside cameras and motion sensors can raise privacy concerns, particularly if video recordings or personal data are stored or shared inappropriately.

Mitigation Steps:

- **Secure Cloud Storage**: If your smart lock system uses cloud storage for videos or images, make sure the storage is encrypted and only accessible to authorized users.
- **Data Retention Policies**: Ensure that any footage from cameras is either deleted after a certain period or stored securely with strict access controls.

- **Disable Features**: If you are concerned about privacy, consider disabling features like facial recognition or disabling cloud storage for recorded footage.

4. Battery Life and Power Failures

Smart locks rely on batteries or a constant power source. A battery failure could prevent the lock from working, or a power outage could lock you out of your home.

Mitigation Steps:

- **Monitor Battery Levels**: Most smart locks have an indicator to show when the battery is low. Regularly check battery levels and replace them as needed.
- **Backup Power Options**: Some smart locks include backup power options (such as a micro-USB port) to power the lock during battery failure.

Conclusion

Smart locks provide enhanced security and convenience by allowing remote access, voice control, and automation of door entry. By integrating smart locks with other IoT devices like security cameras and motion sensors, you can create a highly secure, automated, and efficient system. However, it's crucial to consider the security and privacy concerns associated with smart locks, including potential hacking risks, data breaches, and privacy issues. By implementing strong security measures, keeping software up to date, and following best practices for privacy, you can enjoy the benefits of smart locks while minimizing the risks.

CHAPTER 19

SMART APPLIANCES: CONNECTING KITCHEN AND HOME DEVICES

The modern kitchen is quickly becoming a hub of innovation, where traditional appliances are being transformed into smart devices that can be controlled, monitored, and automated through technology. Integrating devices like **coffee makers**, **microwaves**, **refrigerators**, and other kitchen appliances into your smart home system can greatly enhance convenience, efficiency, and energy management. In this chapter, we'll explore how to integrate smart kitchen appliances using **Raspberry Pi**, automate everyday tasks with sensors, and look at real-world use cases for smart kitchen appliances.

Integrating Devices Like Coffee Makers, Microwaves, and More

Smart kitchen appliances are designed to connect to the internet, enabling you to control them remotely via apps or voice commands. Some devices, like **smart coffee makers**, **microwaves**, and **smart refrigerators**, have built-in connectivity. However, even non-smart appliances can be upgraded to work with a home automation system by using tools like **smart plugs**, **Raspberry Pi**, and **IoT sensors**.

1. Integrating Smart Coffee Makers

Smart coffee makers allow you to brew coffee remotely, set schedules, and even adjust brew strength, temperature, and coffee grind size, all from your smartphone or voice assistant.

Example Integration:

- **Voice Command**: "Alexa, start the coffee maker," or "Google, brew my coffee at 7 AM."
- **App Control**: Control the brewing time, coffee strength, and even get notifications when the coffee is ready.

How to Connect to Raspberry Pi:

To integrate a non-smart coffee maker into your automation system, you can use a **smart plug** to control the power, or integrate a **relay module** with the Raspberry Pi to switch the coffee maker on or off based on scheduled times or sensor data (e.g., when motion is detected in the kitchen).

Example Setup:

1. **Smart Plug**: Plug the coffee maker into a Wi-Fi-enabled smart plug, and use a mobile app to schedule or control the coffee maker remotely.
2. **Relay Module**: If using Raspberry Pi, connect a relay module to the coffee maker and control it through Python scripts or Node-RED.

2. Integrating Smart Microwaves

Smart microwaves come with Wi-Fi capabilities that let you control them remotely, check cooking progress, or adjust settings from an app.

Example Integration:

- **Voice Command**: "Alexa, start heating the leftovers," or "Google, microwave the popcorn for 2 minutes."
- **App Control**: Set specific cooking times, cooking modes, or even track the microwave's usage remotely.

How to Integrate with Raspberry Pi:

You can monitor the microwave's usage or automate the heating process using a **smart plug** and Raspberry Pi, or even automate routines based on time of day.

3. Connecting Smart Refrigerators

Smart refrigerators come equipped with sensors to monitor the temperature, track food inventory, and even alert you when items are running low. They often integrate with apps that let you keep an eye on the contents of your fridge from anywhere.

Example Integration:

- **Voice Command**: "Alexa, what's inside the fridge?" or "Google, set the fridge temperature to 3°C."
- **App Control**: Check the fridge's temperature, inventory, and receive reminders for items that are about to expire.

How to Integrate with Raspberry Pi:

If you want to create a custom smart fridge system using Raspberry Pi, you can integrate **temperature sensors** (e.g., **DHT22**) to monitor the fridge's internal environment, control **smart plugs** to turn appliances like ice makers on/off, or set up **motion sensors** to monitor when the fridge door is opened.

Automating Everyday Tasks Using Sensors and Raspberry Pi

Automating tasks in the kitchen can save time and improve efficiency. With the help of **Raspberry Pi** and **IoT sensors**, you can automate a range of kitchen activities such as monitoring the temperature, controlling appliances based on schedules, and setting up alerts.

1. Motion Sensors for Automated Kitchen Lighting

Using **PIR motion sensors** in the kitchen can help automate the lighting. For example, lights can turn on when someone enters the kitchen and turn off when no motion is detected after a set period.

Example Setup:

1. **PIR Motion Sensor**: Attach the sensor to the kitchen's entrance to detect movement.
2. **Raspberry Pi**: Use the Raspberry Pi to control the light via a relay or GPIO pin.
3. **Automation**: Create a Python script to turn on the light when motion is detected and off after a set period.

2. Temperature Sensors for Smart Cooking

Monitoring the temperature of cooking appliances like ovens, fridges, or coffee makers can help ensure that the cooking process is efficient and that appliances operate within optimal ranges.

Example Setup:

1. **Temperature Sensor (e.g., DHT22)**: Place the sensor near the cooking appliance (e.g., the oven or coffee maker) to monitor temperature.
2. **Automation**: Use the sensor data to turn off the oven when it reaches the desired temperature or send a notification if the coffee maker is ready.

3. Water Flow Sensors for Dishwashers or Faucets

You can integrate **water flow sensors** with Raspberry Pi to monitor water usage in appliances like dishwashers or even water faucets in the kitchen. This setup could help you track water consumption and detect leaks.

Example Setup:

1. **Water Flow Sensor**: Attach the sensor to the dishwasher or faucet.
2. **Raspberry Pi**: Use the Raspberry Pi to monitor the sensor data and send notifications when abnormal water usage is detected, such as leaks or excessive use.

3. **Automation**: Turn off the water supply if a leak is detected.

Real-World Use Cases for Smart Kitchen Appliances

Now that we have discussed how to integrate various kitchen devices, let's explore some real-world use cases where smart kitchen appliances can make everyday tasks easier and more efficient.

1. Smart Coffee Maker Automation

You could set up a smart coffee maker with Raspberry Pi, integrating it with a motion sensor. For instance, the system could detect when someone enters the kitchen in the morning and automatically start brewing coffee. Additionally, the coffee strength could be adjusted based on personal preference stored in the system.

Scenario:

- **Automation**: When motion is detected in the kitchen at 7 AM, the coffee maker starts brewing coffee, and a notification is sent to your phone when the coffee is ready.

- **Voice Control**: Use Alexa to start brewing coffee or adjust the brewing time based on your schedule.

2. Smart Oven with Recipe Suggestions

A smart oven can be integrated with sensors to automatically adjust cooking times and temperatures based on the type of food being cooked. It could also suggest recipes based on the ingredients stored in your fridge.

Scenario:

- **Automation**: Based on voice commands, the smart oven preheats to the required temperature for baking or roasting, and automatically adjusts the time depending on the recipe.
- **Recipe Suggestions**: A Raspberry Pi system integrated with your fridge inventory can suggest recipes and control the oven accordingly.

3. Smart Fridge Inventory Management

Using sensors and a Raspberry Pi, you can monitor the contents of your fridge in real-time. For example, a system could track the expiration dates of items, notify you when something is running low, or automatically add items to a shopping list.

Scenario:

- **Automation**: When a bottle of milk is about to expire, your smart fridge notifies you, and it automatically adds the item to your shopping list on a mobile app.
- **Voice Control**: You can ask Alexa, "What's inside the fridge?" and get a list of the current contents.

4. Energy Efficiency for the Kitchen

By integrating smart plugs and energy monitors with Raspberry Pi, you can track the energy consumption of kitchen appliances. This setup allows you to reduce energy waste by automating the on/off schedule of appliances like the dishwasher or coffee maker, or sending alerts when energy usage exceeds a set threshold.

Scenario:

- **Energy Monitoring**: The system tracks the energy usage of your microwave and sends you an alert if it exceeds a set limit, prompting you to turn off the microwave or adjust your usage patterns.
- **Automation**: Automate turning off the coffee maker after brewing, or schedule the dishwasher to run at night when electricity rates are lower.

Conclusion

Integrating smart kitchen appliances using **Raspberry Pi** and IoT sensors allows you to automate and optimize various kitchen tasks. From controlling coffee makers, ovens, and refrigerators with voice commands, to automating everyday activities like lighting and energy management, smart appliances can transform your kitchen into a more efficient, convenient, and connected space. By leveraging **sensors** and **Raspberry Pi**, you can build customized solutions that enhance your cooking experience, reduce energy waste, and simplify your daily routines, all while maintaining the flexibility and control that come with home automation.

CHAPTER 20

HOME AUTOMATION AND ENERGY EFFICIENCY

Home automation not only enhances convenience and comfort but also provides opportunities for significant energy savings. By integrating IoT sensors and intelligent systems into your home, you can track, manage, and optimize energy consumption, leading to reduced utility bills and a smaller environmental footprint. This chapter will explore how to track and manage energy consumption using IoT sensors, design energy-saving systems with smart plugs and lighting control, and create a green, energy-efficient smart home system.

Tracking and Managing Energy Consumption through IoT Sensors

Tracking and managing energy consumption is the first step towards making your home more energy-efficient. IoT sensors and devices allow you to monitor energy usage in real-time, identify inefficiencies, and optimize your consumption patterns.

1. Energy Monitoring with Smart Plugs

Smart plugs equipped with **energy monitoring features** can be plugged into appliances to track their energy usage. These devices report the energy consumption of individual appliances, which you can monitor through a mobile app or a home automation dashboard.

Example Setup:

1. **Smart Plugs**: Plug your appliances (e.g., TV, refrigerator, coffee maker) into **Wi-Fi-enabled smart plugs** with energy monitoring capabilities.
2. **Energy Monitoring**: Use the app or home automation system to track the energy consumption of each appliance in real-time.
3. **Automation**: Set up routines to automatically turn off appliances when they are not in use, such as turning off a TV after a set period of inactivity.

2. Smart Meters for Whole-Home Monitoring

Smart meters are advanced devices that can monitor the overall energy consumption of your home and send real-time data to your utility provider or home automation system.

Example Setup:

- **Smart Meter**: Install a smart meter in your home's electrical panel to track the overall energy consumption of your entire household.
- **Data Logging**: Use a **Raspberry Pi** or **Home Assistant** to collect data from the smart meter and create visual reports of your energy usage over time.
- **Real-Time Monitoring**: Monitor your energy consumption in real-time and receive alerts when your energy usage exceeds a set threshold.

3. Energy Monitoring Sensors

For more advanced setups, **current sensors** (such as **INA219**) can be used with Raspberry Pi to monitor the energy usage of specific appliances or circuits in your home. These sensors measure the current drawn by appliances and calculate the energy consumption based on voltage and current readings.

Example Setup:

- **Current Sensors**: Install current sensors on power cables connected to specific devices (e.g., HVAC system, lighting circuits).

- **Integration with Raspberry Pi**: Connect the sensors to Raspberry Pi using GPIO pins to monitor the energy consumption in real-time.
- **Data Collection**: Use a Python script to log energy consumption data and display it on a dashboard for easy tracking.

Designing Systems for Energy-Saving (Smart Plugs, Lighting Control)

Once you have a system in place to track energy usage, you can design automated systems to reduce consumption and increase energy efficiency.

1. Smart Plugs for Energy Efficiency

Smart plugs enable remote control of appliances and can help reduce energy consumption by scheduling devices to turn off when not needed or by monitoring their usage patterns.

Example Features of Smart Plugs:

- **Scheduled Control**: Set a schedule for when your appliances should be turned on or off. For instance, you can turn off the coffee maker automatically after 30 minutes.

- **Power Monitoring**: Track the energy consumption of appliances over time to identify high-energy usage and take action to reduce waste.
- **Voice Control**: Use voice assistants like **Alexa** or **Google Assistant** to turn off devices when you leave the house, such as unplugging your iron or TV.

Example Setup:

- **Automating Coffee Maker**: Use a smart plug to turn off the coffee maker after 30 minutes, saving energy that would otherwise be wasted if the device was left on.

2. Lighting Control for Energy Savings

Automating your lighting system is one of the easiest and most effective ways to save energy. Using **smart bulbs** or **smart switches**, you can program your lights to turn off when not needed or adjust their brightness based on ambient light levels.

Example Features:

- **Motion Sensors**: Automate lighting based on motion detection. For example, lights turn on when you enter a room and turn off after a certain period of inactivity.

- **Smart Light Scheduling**: Set up schedules for your lights to turn on or off at certain times, such as turning off lights during the day when natural light is available.
- **Dimmer Controls**: Use dimmer switches or smart bulbs to adjust the brightness of lights based on time of day or room occupancy.

Example Setup:

1. **Smart Bulbs**: Install smart LED bulbs that can be controlled remotely via a smartphone app or integrated with your home automation system.
2. **Motion Sensors**: Install **PIR motion sensors** that trigger lights to turn on when someone enters the room and turn off after a period of inactivity (e.g., 5 minutes).
3. **Daylight Harvesting**: Use a **LUX sensor** to measure natural light levels and adjust artificial lighting accordingly to maintain a desired level of brightness.

3. Thermostats and HVAC Control

Your home's **heating, ventilation, and air conditioning (HVAC)** system is likely one of your largest energy consumers. Smart thermostats allow you to automate temperature settings to optimize energy usage.

Example Features:

- **Adaptive Scheduling**: A smart thermostat learns your schedule and adjusts the temperature accordingly to save energy. For example, it could lower the temperature while you're at work and raise it just before you come home.
- **Geofencing**: Using GPS data, the thermostat can automatically adjust the temperature when you leave or return home.
- **Remote Control**: You can control the temperature remotely from your smartphone, ensuring that energy isn't wasted while you're away.

Example Setup:

- **Smart Thermostat**: Install a **smart thermostat** like the **Nest Thermostat** or **Ecobee** that learns your preferences and adjusts the temperature automatically.
- **Geofencing**: Set up geofencing so that when you leave the house, the thermostat adjusts to a more energy-efficient setting, and when you return, it ensures your home is comfortable.

Building a Green, Energy-Efficient Smart Home System

Building a green, energy-efficient smart home system involves more than just automating individual appliances. It requires integrating various smart systems to optimize energy use throughout the home. Here are some steps to create an energy-efficient system:

1. Use Renewable Energy Sources

If possible, consider integrating **solar panels** or other renewable energy sources into your home. With a solar-powered system, you can use energy-efficient appliances and monitor your energy production and consumption in real-time.

Example Setup:

- **Solar Panels**: Install solar panels on your roof and connect them to a **solar inverter** to manage energy flow.
- **Energy Monitoring**: Use an energy monitoring system to track both your solar energy production and household consumption, adjusting appliance use to maximize solar power usage during peak sunlight hours.

2. Whole-Home Energy Management System

A **whole-home energy management system** can track and control the energy consumption of every device in your home. This system can integrate smart thermostats, lights, plugs, and even appliances like refrigerators to ensure that energy is being used efficiently.

Example Setup:

- **Home Automation Hub**: Use a **Raspberry Pi** or **Home Assistant** as a central hub to manage all your smart devices.
- **Energy Monitoring Integration**: Integrate energy monitoring sensors into the system to track energy usage in real-time.
- **Optimized Scheduling**: Automatically schedule appliances like washing machines or dishwashers to run at off-peak hours, saving on electricity costs.

3. Water Conservation

In addition to managing energy, smart homes can also be designed to conserve water. Using IoT sensors and devices such as **smart faucets**, **irrigation systems**, and **water meters** can help reduce water wastage.

Example Setup:

- **Smart Irrigation**: Use **soil moisture sensors** and **smart irrigation controllers** to water plants only when necessary, saving both water and energy.
- **Smart Faucets**: Install **smart faucets** that automatically adjust water flow based on usage or turn off when the faucet has been idle for a period of time.

Conclusion

Building a green, energy-efficient smart home involves integrating smart appliances, sensors, and systems that track, monitor, and optimize energy consumption. By using **smart plugs**, **lighting control**, **thermostats**, and **energy monitoring sensors**, you can reduce your household's energy usage, lower costs, and contribute to a more sustainable future. Whether you're automating lighting, controlling HVAC systems, or managing energy with IoT sensors, the integration of home automation and energy efficiency can make your home more comfortable, convenient, and eco-friendly.

CHAPTER 21

ADVANCED HOME AUTOMATION: MULTI-ROOM AUDIO SYSTEMS

A multi-room audio system brings the power of music, podcasts, and other audio content to every corner of your home. Whether you want to play music in the kitchen while cooking, in the living room during a party, or in the bedroom to relax, a well-designed multi-room audio system can create an immersive, convenient experience. In this chapter, we will explore how to create a **multi-room audio system** using **Raspberry Pi**, integrate various speakers and media controllers, and automate music playback with room-specific control.

Creating a Multi-Room Audio System with Raspberry Pi

The versatility of **Raspberry Pi** makes it an ideal platform for building a custom multi-room audio system. By installing open-source software like **Volumio**, **RuneAudio**, or **Pi MusicBox**, you can turn each Raspberry Pi into a media player capable of streaming audio to connected speakers.

1. Setting Up Raspberry Pi for Audio Playback

To begin, you will need a **Raspberry Pi**, a microSD card with the desired audio software installed, and a way to connect your Raspberry Pi to your speakers.

Components Needed:

- **Raspberry Pi** (Model 3 or 4 is recommended)
- **MicroSD Card** (8GB or larger)
- **Speakers** (wired or Bluetooth)
- **Power Supply** for Raspberry Pi
- **Audio Software** (e.g., Volumio, RuneAudio, Pi MusicBox)
- **Wi-Fi or Ethernet** for network connectivity

Steps for Setting Up:

1. **Install Audio Software**: Choose an audio management software like **Volumio** and download the latest version from the Volumio website. Flash the software to the microSD card using **Etcher** or any other flashing tool.

2. **Set Up Raspberry Pi**: Insert the microSD card into the Raspberry Pi, connect the Raspberry Pi to a monitor (optional), and power it up.

3. **Connect Speakers**: You can connect the speakers directly via the 3.5mm audio jack or use Bluetooth for wireless speakers. If you are using multiple speakers in different rooms, you can either use **Bluetooth** speakers or connect via **Wi-Fi** through networked devices.

4. **Network Configuration**: Connect the Raspberry Pi to your local network (Wi-Fi or Ethernet). This allows all Raspberry Pis in the system to communicate with each other and stream music seamlessly across rooms.

2. Setting Up Multiple Raspberry Pis

To create a multi-room audio system, set up **multiple Raspberry Pi** devices, one in each room. Each Raspberry Pi will act as an independent audio player that can be controlled from a central interface.

Example Setup:

1. **Raspberry Pi in the Living Room**: Connect one Raspberry Pi to the speakers in the living room.

2. **Raspberry Pi in the Kitchen**: Set up another Raspberry Pi in the kitchen, connected to Bluetooth or wired speakers.

3. **Raspberry Pi in the Bedroom**: Place another Raspberry Pi in the bedroom and connect it to the speakers.

3. Synchronizing Audio Across Rooms

To synchronize audio across rooms, you can use network-based protocols like **AirPlay** (for Apple devices) or **Snapcast** (for multi-room audio using **Raspberry Pi**).

Example Software Solutions:

- **Snapcast**: This open-source server/client system can synchronize multiple Raspberry Pi devices, allowing them to play audio in sync. You can control each Raspberry Pi's audio output, and they will all play the same audio simultaneously in different rooms.
- **AirPlay**: If you have Apple devices or are using **AirPlay**-compatible software (such as **Shairport Sync**), you can stream music from your Apple device to multiple Raspberry Pi audio players at once.

Integrating Speakers, Media Controllers, and Streaming Services

Once your **multi-room audio system** is set up, you can integrate speakers, media controllers, and streaming services to complete the system. This will allow you to control audio playback, select music, and stream content seamlessly.

1. Integrating Speakers

You have multiple options for integrating speakers into your multi-room audio system:

- **Wired Speakers**: Use the Raspberry Pi's 3.5mm audio jack or **USB sound card** to connect wired speakers directly to the Raspberry Pi. You can control audio playback via the software interface.
- **Bluetooth Speakers**: For flexibility, you can pair each Raspberry Pi with Bluetooth speakers. Most audio software (e.g., Volumio, RuneAudio) supports Bluetooth audio output.
- **Wi-Fi Speakers**: Some advanced systems support Wi-Fi speakers, which can be connected via **AirPlay**, **Spotify Connect**, or other network protocols.

2. Integrating Media Controllers

A **media controller** allows you to control the audio playback across rooms from a single device, such as a smartphone, tablet, or computer.

Example Controller Integration:

- **Volumio Web Interface**: Volumio provides a web-based interface where you can control each Raspberry Pi's audio output, choose songs, and manage volume.
- **Smartphone App**: Many Raspberry Pi audio software solutions have companion apps that allow you to control the audio playback remotely from your smartphone. For instance, you can use **Volumio's mobile app** to control your music.

3. Integrating Streaming Services

To stream music from popular services like **Spotify**, **Tidal**, or **Apple Music**, you need to integrate these services with your audio software.

Example Setup:

- **Spotify**: Most Raspberry Pi audio software supports **Spotify Connect**, allowing you to stream music directly from the Spotify app to your Raspberry Pi devices. This can be controlled from your phone or computer.
- **AirPlay**: If you are using AirPlay-enabled devices, you can stream from **Apple Music** or any other app that supports AirPlay.

- **Pandora or Other Services**: Some services can be integrated through browser extensions or apps on the Raspberry Pi.

Automating Music Play and Room-Specific Control

With automation, you can set up the system to play music based on specific conditions such as time of day, occupancy, or room preferences. Raspberry Pi and IoT sensors can work together to create an automated, hands-free experience for your multi-room audio system.

1. Automating Music Play

You can automate music play by setting up triggers based on time, events, or sensor data:

- **Time-Based Automation**: Set up a schedule for playing music at certain times of the day. For example, you could schedule relaxing music to play in the living room every evening at 6 PM.
- **Sensor-Based Automation**: Use **motion sensors** (PIR) or **contact sensors** (on doors) to trigger music when someone enters a room. For instance, when you enter the kitchen in the morning, your Raspberry Pi system can

automatically start playing your favorite breakfast playlist.

- **Voice Control**: Integrate with voice assistants like **Amazon Alexa** or **Google Assistant** to control music playback hands-free. You can say, "Alexa, play jazz in the living room," or "Hey Google, play morning music in the kitchen."

2. Room-Specific Control

With a multi-room audio setup, you can customize audio playback in each room.

- **Individual Volume Control**: Control the volume in each room separately, allowing for different listening levels depending on room size or activity. For example, you can have a louder volume in the living room for a party while keeping the bedroom volume low for background music.
- **Room-Specific Playlists**: Set up different playlists for different rooms, such as relaxing music in the bedroom and upbeat tunes in the kitchen.
- **Smart Sensing**: Use **motion sensors** and **presence sensors** to automate room-specific music play. For instance, music starts playing when someone enters the living room, but it turns off automatically when the room is empty.

Real-World Use Cases for Multi-Room Audio Systems

Here are a few real-world scenarios where multi-room audio systems come in handy:

1. House Party or Gathering

During a party, you can synchronize music across multiple rooms. Set up the system to play the same music in all rooms, or tailor it to different areas. For example:

- **Living Room**: Play upbeat, dance music.
- **Kitchen**: Play background music for conversations.
- **Bedroom**: Play relaxing tunes or ambient sounds.

2. Morning Routine

Set up an automated routine where the system starts playing the **news** or your favorite **morning playlist** when you enter the kitchen or bathroom. The music can be synced across all rooms to provide a consistent experience throughout the home.

3. Relaxing in the Evening

At the end of the day, you can have calming music or ambient sounds playing in the bedroom or living room as part of your winding-down routine. You can set it to start automatically based on a schedule or a voice command.

Conclusion

Creating a **multi-room audio system** with **Raspberry Pi** opens up endless possibilities for enhancing your home entertainment experience. Whether you're listening to music, podcasts, or audiobooks, you can automate audio playback, control volume across rooms, and integrate smart devices like motion sensors, speakers, and media controllers to create a seamless experience. By using open-source software, integrating streaming services, and automating based on time or room-specific conditions, you can transform your home into a dynamic, connected space that adapts to your lifestyle.

CHAPTER 22

MANAGING SMART HOMES WITH MOBILE APPLICATIONS

In the age of connectivity, managing your smart home remotely has become a powerful tool for convenience, efficiency, and security. Mobile applications serve as the bridge between users and their smart home systems, enabling control over devices, automation, and monitoring from virtually anywhere. This chapter will explore how to develop mobile apps to manage your smart home, using frameworks like **Flutter** or **React Native** to create cross-platform applications. We'll also look at how to integrate these apps with IoT devices and **Raspberry Pi** for a seamless, interactive experience.

Developing Mobile Apps to Control Your Smart Home from Anywhere

Creating a mobile app to control your smart home gives you the freedom to manage devices, automate tasks, and monitor the status of appliances from any location. Whether you're at work, on vacation, or in bed, mobile apps bring the power of smart home management directly to your fingertips.

1. Key Features for a Smart Home Mobile App

A well-designed mobile app for smart homes should offer features that give users full control and visibility over their home automation system. Some of the essential features include:

- **Device Control**: Ability to turn devices on/off, adjust settings (e.g., lights, thermostats), and monitor device status (e.g., whether a door is locked or a light is on).
- **Automation and Scheduling**: Set schedules for when devices should operate, such as turning lights on at sunset or adjusting the thermostat in the morning.
- **Notifications**: Receive real-time notifications about events like motion detection, door opening, or changes in temperature.
- **Voice Control**: Integration with voice assistants like Alexa, Google Assistant, or Siri for hands-free control.
- **Energy Monitoring**: Track energy usage for devices like smart plugs, thermostats, and appliances.
- **Security Features**: Monitor cameras, locks, and sensors for security, and receive alerts if any suspicious activity is detected.

2. Choosing the Right Mobile Development Framework

When building a mobile app for smart home management, selecting the right development framework is crucial for ensuring cross-platform compatibility and fast development cycles. Two of the most popular frameworks are **Flutter** and **React Native**, both of which allow you to create mobile apps for both **iOS** and **Android** from a single codebase.

Using Flutter or React Native to Create Cross-Platform Smart Home Apps

Both **Flutter** and **React Native** are great choices for building mobile apps with a unified codebase for both Android and iOS platforms. Here's a breakdown of these frameworks and how they can help you develop smart home apps.

1. Flutter: Cross-Platform Development with a Rich UI

Flutter, developed by Google, is a UI toolkit that allows developers to create natively compiled applications for mobile, web, and desktop from a single codebase. It's known for its fast development cycle and high-performance rendering engine, making it an excellent choice for building smart home apps with complex, interactive UIs.

Benefits of Using Flutter for Smart Home Apps:

- **Hot Reload**: The ability to instantly see changes in the app's UI during development, which speeds up the development process.
- **Customizable Widgets**: Flutter offers a wide range of customizable widgets, which allows you to create a unique and visually appealing user interface for controlling your smart home.
- **Performance**: Flutter's direct compilation to native code ensures that your app performs well on both Android and iOS devices, even with complex features like real-time device control.

Example Features in Flutter:

- **Device Control UI**: Use Flutter's widget system to create clean, responsive interfaces for controlling lights, temperature, and other smart home devices.
- **Integration with APIs**: Use **Flutter plugins** to integrate with APIs for controlling IoT devices (e.g., **MQTT** or **REST APIs** for communication with your Raspberry Pi).
- **Notifications**: Use Flutter's **Firebase Cloud Messaging (FCM)** or other notification services to alert users about device status changes, energy usage, or security events.

2. React Native: Building Native-Like Apps with JavaScript

React Native is a popular framework developed by Facebook for building mobile apps using JavaScript and React. It's known for allowing developers to create apps with near-native performance while using a single codebase for both Android and iOS platforms.

Benefits of Using React Native for Smart Home Apps:

- **Reusable Components**: React Native's component-based architecture makes it easy to reuse code across different parts of the app, saving development time.
- **Strong Ecosystem**: React Native has a large and mature ecosystem of libraries and tools that can help with integrating IoT devices, managing state, and handling complex app logic.
- **Community Support**: Being one of the most widely used frameworks, React Native has strong community support, making it easy to find resources and troubleshoot issues.

Example Features in React Native:

- **Real-Time Device Control**: Use **React Native WebSocket** or **MQTT** to create real-time device control, allowing users to turn devices on or off without refreshing the app.

223

- **User Authentication**: Implement user authentication with services like **Firebase Authentication** to allow users to securely access and control their smart home.
- **Smart Home Dashboard**: Build a dashboard where users can monitor the status of all their devices, with real-time updates, using **React Navigation** for smooth navigation between different views.

Integration with IoT Devices and Raspberry Pi

Once you've built the app, the next step is integrating it with **IoT devices** and **Raspberry Pi**. The Raspberry Pi can serve as the central hub of your smart home, controlling devices such as lights, thermostats, sensors, and cameras. The mobile app will communicate with Raspberry Pi via APIs, allowing users to control and monitor their devices.

1. Connecting Raspberry Pi to IoT Devices

To integrate IoT devices with Raspberry Pi, you can use different communication protocols such as **MQTT, HTTP REST APIs**, or **WebSockets**. Raspberry Pi can communicate with sensors, smart plugs, and other devices either directly or through an intermediary like **Home Assistant** or **OpenHAB**.

Example Setup for Raspberry Pi and IoT Devices:

- **MQTT Broker**: Set up an MQTT broker on the Raspberry Pi to allow communication with devices like lights, motion sensors, and thermostats.
- **IoT Devices**: Use Raspberry Pi GPIO pins to interface with sensors or relays (e.g., controlling lights or security cameras).
- **App Communication**: The mobile app communicates with Raspberry Pi using **HTTP requests** or **MQTT** to control devices, fetch sensor data, or trigger automation routines.

2. Using REST APIs for Communication

If you are using a platform like **Home Assistant** or **OpenHAB** on your Raspberry Pi, these platforms typically offer **REST APIs** that allow you to interact with your devices. Your mobile app can send HTTP requests to these APIs to control devices or fetch data.

Example Communication via REST API:

1. **GET Request**: Retrieve data about the status of a device, like the current temperature from a thermostat.

   ```
   javascript
   ```

```
fetch('http://<raspberry-pi-
ip>:8123/api/states/sensor.temperature', {
  method: 'GET',
  headers: {
    'Authorization':    'Bearer    <access-
token>',
  }
})
.then(response => response.json())
.then(data => console.log(data));
```

2. **POST Request**: Send a command to turn on a light or adjust the thermostat.

```javascript
fetch('http://<raspberry-pi-
ip>:8123/api/services/light/turn_on', {
  method: 'POST',
  headers: {
    'Authorization':    'Bearer    <access-
token>',
    'Content-Type': 'application/json',
  },
  body: JSON.stringify({
    entity_id: 'light.living_room',
  })
})
.then(response => response.json())
.then(data => console.log(data));
```

Conclusion

Developing mobile apps to manage your smart home with **Flutter** or **React Native** provides a powerful way to control and monitor IoT devices remotely, offering flexibility and convenience. By integrating with **Raspberry Pi** and other IoT devices, you can create an automated, connected home system that allows users to interact with devices through their smartphones from anywhere. Whether using **MQTT**, **REST APIs**, or **WebSockets** to communicate with the Raspberry Pi, the possibilities for building and customizing a smart home app are vast, enabling you to design solutions that cater to your needs and preferences. With these tools, you can bring your smart home vision to life, making it more intuitive, efficient, and connected.

CHAPTER 23
TROUBLESHOOTING AND MAINTAINING YOUR SMART HOME

As your smart home becomes more complex with the integration of IoT devices and automation systems, it's inevitable that you may encounter occasional issues. Troubleshooting and maintaining your system are essential to ensure everything works smoothly. This chapter will cover the common issues in smart home systems, how to fix them, best practices for long-term maintenance of IoT-based systems, and crucial steps for securing your network and updating software regularly.

Common Issues in Smart Home Systems and How to Fix Them

While smart home devices are designed to work seamlessly, issues can arise due to network problems, software glitches, or hardware malfunctions. Below are some common issues you may face and steps to resolve them.

1. Device Connectivity Issues

One of the most frequent problems in smart homes is that devices often disconnect from the network or fail to communicate with each other.

Troubleshooting Steps:

- **Check Network Connection**: Ensure your Wi-Fi or Ethernet connection is stable. If devices are on different networks, ensure they are connected to the same network or that your router settings support inter-device communication.
- **Restart Devices**: Sometimes simply restarting the device or rebooting the **Raspberry Pi** can resolve connectivity issues.
- **Re-pair Devices**: If your devices use Bluetooth or Zigbee, they might lose connection. Re-pair the devices by following the manufacturer's instructions.
- **Signal Range**: Ensure that devices such as **smart plugs**, **sensors**, or **light bulbs** are within the range of your router or the device's wireless signal. You may need a **Wi-Fi extender** or **Zigbee repeater** to boost the signal range.

2. Smart Home Devices Not Responding

Occasionally, your smart home devices might stop responding to commands, either from the mobile app or voice assistants like **Alexa** or **Google Assistant**.

Troubleshooting Steps:

- **Check Device Power**: Ensure the devices are powered on and that there are no power issues (e.g., low batteries in sensors or devices).

- **Reset the Device**: For devices that aren't responding, try resetting them by following the manufacturer's reset instructions, often involving holding a button or toggling the power.

- **Check the App or Integration**: If you're using a home automation hub (like **Home Assistant** or **SmartThings**), ensure the app or system is properly synced and that all devices are listed and connected.

- **Reconfigure Automations**: If automations aren't working as expected, double-check the configurations in your mobile app or automation platform. Make sure the triggers and actions are set up correctly.

3. Latency or Delayed Responses

Sometimes, IoT devices might experience latency, where commands take a long time to execute or don't respond immediately.

Troubleshooting Steps:

- **Reduce Network Traffic**: Ensure your network isn't overloaded with traffic from other devices. You may need to prioritize IoT traffic or use a separate network for IoT devices.
- **Use Wired Connections**: For critical devices (e.g., hubs or Raspberry Pi), using **Ethernet** instead of Wi-Fi can reduce latency and improve response times.
- **Optimize Device Placement**: Poor placement of Wi-Fi or Zigbee devices might cause delays. Ensure that devices are placed within the effective range of your router or network coordinator.

4. Compatibility Problems

As you integrate different devices from multiple manufacturers, compatibility issues may arise. Not all IoT devices are compatible with each other, and some may require specific hubs or apps to function.

Troubleshooting Steps:

- **Use Compatible Hubs**: Ensure that your smart devices are compatible with the platform or hub you're using. Platforms like **Google Home, Apple HomeKit**, and **Amazon Alexa** support a wide range of devices, but compatibility checks are essential before purchasing new devices.
- **Firmware Updates**: Check for firmware updates for devices or hubs, as updates can fix compatibility problems and improve overall performance.
- **Check API or Service Support**: If using third-party services (like **IFTTT**), make sure they support the IoT devices you are trying to integrate.

Best Practices for Long-Term Maintenance of IoT-Based Systems

A smart home system requires ongoing maintenance to ensure its long-term performance, security, and reliability. Following best practices will help keep your smart home running smoothly.

1. Keep Software and Firmware Updated

Regularly updating the software and firmware of your devices ensures that you benefit from bug fixes, new features, and security improvements.

Tips for Updates:

- **Enable Automatic Updates**: Where possible, enable automatic updates for devices and apps to ensure that you are always running the latest versions.
- **Check for Manual Updates**: For devices like Raspberry Pi, smart thermostats, or security cameras, check for updates manually via the device's app or web interface.
- **Monitor Release Notes**: Check the release notes for updates to understand what changes have been made, including bug fixes or new features that could affect your setup.

2. Regularly Backup Your Smart Home System

Backing up your home automation setup ensures that, in case of a system failure or reset, you can restore your configuration and minimize downtime.

Tips for Backups:

- **Backup Configuration Files**: If using **Home Assistant** or similar platforms, back up your configuration files regularly to ensure you can restore settings quickly.
- **Backup Device Data**: For security cameras or video doorbells, back up critical footage if cloud storage isn't an option. Use an external storage device or cloud services for long-term backup.

3. Regularly Clean Devices and Maintain Hardware

Physical maintenance of devices is just as important as software maintenance.

Tips for Hardware Maintenance:

- **Clean Devices**: Dust and dirt can affect the performance of sensors and cameras. Clean the lenses of cameras, and wipe down devices regularly.
- **Replace Batteries**: For battery-operated devices like door sensors or smart locks, replace the batteries as needed. Some systems offer low battery alerts, but it's good practice to check periodically.
- **Test Devices**: Periodically check that all devices are functioning correctly. This includes testing the connection, sensors, and control systems.

4. Monitor Device Health

Keep an eye on the health and performance of critical devices like smart thermostats, security cameras, and hubs.

Monitoring Tips:

- **Health Dashboard**: Some smart home platforms provide dashboards that show the health and status of all devices. This can help you identify devices that need attention or aren't working as expected.
- **System Logs**: Review system logs for unusual behavior or errors that could indicate hardware malfunctions or software issues.

Securing Your Network and Updating Software Regularly

The security of your smart home system is paramount to protect against potential breaches, hacking attempts, or unauthorized access. Regularly securing your network and updating your software will help keep your smart home safe.

1. Secure Your Home Network

IoT devices are often the target of cyberattacks, so ensuring your network is secure is a critical part of maintaining your smart home.

Network Security Tips:

- **Use Strong Passwords**: Ensure that all devices, apps, and hubs are protected by strong, unique passwords. Avoid using default credentials.
- **Enable Encryption**: Use WPA3 encryption for your Wi-Fi network, and ensure IoT devices that communicate over the internet (e.g., cameras, smart locks) use encrypted connections (SSL/TLS).
- **Segment Your Network**: Consider setting up a **separate Wi-Fi network** for IoT devices to isolate them from your personal computers and phones, reducing the potential attack surface.
- **Use VPNs**: Consider using a **VPN** for remote access to your smart home, particularly if you control it through the internet.

2. Regular Software Updates for Security

Keep your devices up-to-date to patch known vulnerabilities and avoid security exploits.

Software Security Tips:

- **Enable Automatic Software Updates**: For devices like smart thermostats, cameras, and home automation hubs, ensure that software updates are applied automatically whenever possible.
- **Update Raspberry Pi Software**: If you are using **Raspberry Pi** for home automation, run regular updates by executing the following commands:

bash

```
sudo apt-get update
sudo apt-get upgrade
```

- **Security Patches**: Check for security patches regularly, especially for devices with internet-facing services (e.g., security cameras, smart locks).

3. Monitor and Audit Access

Regularly review who has access to your smart home system to ensure that only authorized users have control.

Tips for Auditing Access:

- **User Permissions**: For apps and systems that allow multiple users (e.g., shared access), regularly review user permissions and ensure that only necessary users have access.

- **Use Multi-Factor Authentication (MFA)**: Enable **MFA** for accounts that support it, especially for platforms like **Home Assistant**, **Nest**, or **Amazon Alexa** to add an extra layer of security.

Conclusion

Troubleshooting and maintaining a smart home involves proactive monitoring, regular software updates, and ensuring network security. By addressing common issues such as connectivity problems, device malfunctions, and compatibility challenges, you can keep your smart home running smoothly. Adopting best practices for long-term maintenance, including regular backups and hardware upkeep, will extend the life of your system. Above all, securing your network and keeping software up to date are critical to protecting your smart home from potential threats. With these strategies in place, you'll ensure that your smart home remains efficient, secure, and reliable for years to come.

CHAPTER 24

ADDING AUTOMATION WITH AI AND MACHINE LEARNING

Integrating **AI** and **Machine Learning (ML)** into your smart home system takes automation to the next level by enabling devices to predict needs, adapt to behaviors, and make intelligent decisions based on real-time data. Instead of relying on fixed schedules or simple rules, AI and ML allow your smart home to learn from your habits, preferences, and environmental factors, ultimately providing a more personalized and efficient living experience. In this chapter, we'll explore how AI can automate tasks such as temperature control and light adjustments, use machine learning models to learn user behavior, and provide real-world examples of AI integration in smart homes.

Using AI to Predict and Automate Tasks (e.g., Temperature Control, Light Adjustments)

AI can be used to enhance home automation by enabling systems to predict needs and automatically adjust settings based on learned patterns, context, and environmental factors. Let's explore how this works in different areas of the smart home.

1. Temperature Control

AI-powered smart thermostats, like **Nest** or **Ecobee**, use machine learning algorithms to learn your schedule and temperature preferences over time. Rather than manually adjusting the thermostat every day, these devices can automatically optimize your home's climate.

How It Works:

- **Learning User Behavior**: The thermostat tracks your activities, such as when you're home, when you leave, and your preferred temperature settings at different times of the day.
- **Predictive Adjustments**: AI algorithms predict when the home will be occupied and adjust the temperature accordingly. For example, the thermostat may lower the temperature when you leave for work and begin warming the house up shortly before you return.
- **Energy Optimization**: The system can also adjust to external factors, such as weather forecasts, to optimize energy use. For instance, if a particularly hot day is predicted, the thermostat can start cooling the home earlier to avoid overburdening the system.

Real-World Example:

- **Nest Thermostat** learns the user's preferred temperatures and adjusts heating and cooling automatically based on the time of day, occupancy, and even outside weather conditions, ultimately saving energy and providing comfort without user intervention.

2. Lighting Adjustments

AI can also automate light adjustments based on occupancy, time of day, or environmental factors, making the lighting system more efficient and personalized.

How It Works:

- **Adaptive Lighting**: AI can learn the typical usage patterns of lighting in each room. For example, it may adjust lighting based on when rooms are occupied or when natural light is available.
- **Ambient Lighting**: Using data from light sensors, AI can adjust the brightness and color temperature of lights to suit the time of day or activities. For instance, the lights may gradually brighten in the morning to simulate natural sunrise or dim in the evening for relaxation.

241

Real-World Example:

- **Philips Hue** and **LIFX** smart bulbs use AI to learn user preferences, adjusting lighting based on time of day, occupancy, and even external weather conditions. These bulbs can also integrate with voice assistants like **Alexa** or **Google Assistant**, enabling voice commands to adjust lighting based on the user's current mood or activity.

Machine Learning Models for Learning User Behavior

Machine learning allows your smart home system to continuously improve and adapt to your behavior, making it smarter over time. By analyzing data from IoT devices, such as sensors, cameras, and thermostats, machine learning models can learn patterns and predict what actions to take in different situations.

1. Learning Daily Routines

Machine learning models can analyze the way you interact with your home and predict your preferences. For example, by analyzing your daily routine, the system can learn when you wake up, when you leave for work, and when you typically come home. With this data, the smart home system can anticipate your needs and automatically adjust devices like lights, thermostats, and security systems.

Example Setup:

- **Training the Model**: The system tracks your behavior over a period of time, such as when lights are turned on or off, the temperature settings, and when doors are locked or unlocked.
- **Prediction**: Once enough data is collected, the system can start predicting when certain actions should be performed. For example, if the model detects that you typically leave the house at 8 AM, it can automatically adjust the thermostat and lock the door at that time.

2. Adaptive Security Systems

Machine learning can also improve security by learning normal behavior patterns and detecting anomalies. For example, motion sensors combined with ML algorithms can learn typical patterns of movement around the house and raise an alert if unusual activity is detected (e.g., if a door is opened at an unexpected time or motion is detected in an unusual location).

Example Setup:

- **Training the Model**: Cameras and motion sensors learn what normal activity looks like in your home. For instance, the system may know that you typically move between the kitchen and living room during the evening.
- **Anomaly Detection**: If an unexpected event occurs, such as someone entering the house when no one is expected, the system can raise an alert and send notifications to your phone or smart devices.

Real-World Examples of AI Integration in Smart Homes

The integration of AI into smart home systems can lead to more intelligent and personalized automation. Below are a few real-world examples of how AI is used to enhance the functionality of smart homes.

1. AI in Smart Thermostats

AI-driven thermostats like **Nest** and **Ecobee** provide predictive heating and cooling by learning your preferences and adapting to your daily routine. These thermostats use machine learning to analyze your habits and adjust temperature settings based on real-time data, such as the weather forecast and occupancy.

How It Works:

- **Nest** learns when you're home or away, adjusting the temperature accordingly, and predicting when you'll need heating or cooling. The thermostat can even suggest energy-saving tips based on your habits and the outside temperature.

2. AI-Driven Voice Assistants

Voice assistants like **Amazon Alexa**, **Google Assistant**, and **Apple Siri** rely heavily on AI and machine learning to understand user commands and provide contextual responses. These assistants can integrate with various smart home devices to automate tasks and control your home environment using voice commands.

Example Features:

- **Voice Control**: AI understands natural language commands like "Alexa, turn off the kitchen lights" or "Hey Google, set the thermostat to 72°F."
- **Contextual Awareness**: AI can learn contextual information, such as your location in the house, and

automatically adjust settings. For example, it may automatically turn off lights in rooms you are no longer in.

3. AI for Smart Lighting and Ambience Control

AI-based systems in smart lighting (e.g., **Philips Hue**, **LIFX**) can adjust lighting based on time of day, ambient light levels, or specific user activities, such as watching TV or reading. Machine learning models can learn your lighting preferences over time and automatically adjust lights for comfort or energy savings.

Example Features:

- **Ambient Lighting**: The system adjusts lighting brightness and color temperature based on time of day. In the morning, it may use cooler, brighter lights to wake you up, and at night, it may shift to warmer, dimmer lights for relaxation.
- **Voice or App Control**: Adjust lighting with voice commands or through a mobile app, such as "Hey Google, dim the lights in the living room."

4. Smart Security Cameras and Surveillance

AI-powered cameras like **Nest Cam** and **Ring** use machine learning to detect faces, recognize familiar people, and differentiate between humans, pets, and objects. These cameras can send you alerts based on unusual activity, improving the security of your home.

Example Features:

- **Face Recognition**: AI analyzes faces captured by the camera to identify familiar people, reducing false alerts from pets or non-threatening movements.
- **Activity Zones**: With machine learning, the camera can focus on specific areas (e.g., doorways or windows) and ignore irrelevant parts of the image, improving detection accuracy.

Conclusion

Integrating **AI** and **Machine Learning** into your smart home system enables devices to learn from your behavior, predict your needs, and automate tasks with a level of intelligence and adaptability that goes beyond simple scheduled routines. From **predictive temperature control** and **adaptive lighting** to **intelligent security systems** and personalized automation, AI and ML are transforming how we interact with our homes. By using these technologies, smart homes become more efficient, energy-saving, and capable of offering a deeply personalized user experience. The continuous learning capabilities of AI ensure that as your habits evolve, so will the smart home, making it even smarter and more intuitive over time.

CHAPTER 25

SMART HOME HUBS AND PLATFORMS

Smart home hubs and platforms are the backbone of modern home automation systems. They serve as the central control point, allowing multiple smart devices from different manufacturers to communicate and work together seamlessly. In this chapter, we will explore different smart home hubs and platforms, such as **Home Assistant** and **OpenHAB**, and explain how to set up and use these hubs with **Raspberry Pi**. Additionally, we'll discuss the benefits of using an all-in-one smart home platform for efficient home automation.

Exploring Different Smart Home Hubs (Home Assistant, OpenHAB, etc.)

Smart home hubs allow you to manage various devices in your home from a single platform. These platforms enable seamless integration and control of IoT devices, regardless of the manufacturer. Let's look at a couple of the most popular smart home hubs: **Home Assistant** and **OpenHAB**.

1. Home Assistant

Home Assistant is one of the most widely used open-source smart home platforms. It offers a powerful and flexible system for automating and controlling your devices. Home Assistant runs on various devices, including **Raspberry Pi**, and integrates with a wide range of devices and services.

Key Features:

- **Wide Device Compatibility**: Home Assistant supports over 1,500 integrations with smart devices, including lights, thermostats, cameras, locks, and more.
- **Local Control**: Unlike many commercial systems, Home Assistant runs entirely on your local network, ensuring better privacy and reliability.
- **Automation and Scripting**: Home Assistant allows you to create advanced automation routines and scripts to control your devices based on triggers like time, location, or sensor data.
- **Voice Assistant Integration**: Home Assistant can integrate with **Amazon Alexa**, **Google Assistant**, and **Siri**, allowing for voice control of your devices.

Ideal for:

- Users who prefer an open-source, highly customizable smart home platform.
- Those who want full control of their data and prefer local-only control without relying on cloud services.

2. OpenHAB

OpenHAB (Open Home Automation Bus) is another open-source platform for integrating various smart home devices into a unified system. Like Home Assistant, OpenHAB is flexible, highly customizable, and supports a wide variety of devices.

Key Features:

- **Universal Compatibility**: OpenHAB supports a large number of devices and communication protocols, such as Z-Wave, Zigbee, MQTT, and more.
- **Extensive Rules Engine**: OpenHAB provides a powerful rules engine that lets you create complex automation scripts based on triggers, conditions, and actions.
- **User Interface**: OpenHAB comes with web-based dashboards that can be accessed from any device, allowing you to control your smart home remotely.

- **Voice Assistant Integration**: OpenHAB integrates with voice assistants like **Amazon Alexa** and **Google Assistant** for hands-free control.

Ideal for:

- Users who want a platform with extensive community support and a broad range of device integrations.
- Those who want to create complex automation rules and have a high degree of flexibility.

Setting Up and Using Smart Home Hubs with Raspberry Pi

Both **Home Assistant** and **OpenHAB** can be installed on a **Raspberry Pi** to create a smart home hub. The Raspberry Pi is an excellent choice because of its low cost, small form factor, and ability to run Linux-based operating systems.

1. Setting Up Home Assistant on Raspberry Pi

Here's a step-by-step guide to setting up Home Assistant on your Raspberry Pi:

Step 1: Prepare the Raspberry Pi

- **Download Home Assistant OS**: Go to the Home Assistant website and download the latest version of **Home Assistant OS**.
- **Flash the Image**: Use **Balena Etcher** to flash the Home Assistant OS image onto your **microSD card** (8GB or larger).
- **Insert the microSD Card**: Once flashed, insert the microSD card into the Raspberry Pi.

Step 2: Install Home Assistant

- **Power the Raspberry Pi**: Plug in the Raspberry Pi and power it on.
- **Access Home Assistant**: On your computer or smartphone, open a browser and go to `http://homeassistant.local:8123` or use the Pi's IP address.
- **Complete Setup**: Follow the on-screen instructions to complete the initial setup. You'll need to create a Home Assistant account, configure your location, and start adding devices.

Step 3: Add Devices and Automate

- **Integrate Devices**: You can start adding devices like lights, thermostats, cameras, and sensors. Home Assistant supports hundreds of integrations, either natively or through third-party add-ons.
- **Create Automations**: Use the Home Assistant interface to create automations, such as turning on the lights when motion is detected or adjusting the thermostat when you leave home.

2. Setting Up OpenHAB on Raspberry Pi

Here's how you can install and set up OpenHAB on your Raspberry Pi:

Step 1: Install OpenHAB on Raspberry Pi

- **Download the Image**: Go to the OpenHAB website and download the latest **openHABian** image for Raspberry Pi.
- **Flash the Image**: Use **Balena Etcher** to flash the **openHABian** image onto the microSD card.
- **Insert the microSD Card**: Insert the card into your Raspberry Pi.

Step 2: Set Up OpenHAB

- **Boot the Raspberry Pi**: Power up the Raspberry Pi and wait for it to boot.
- **Access the Interface**: Open a browser on your computer or smartphone and go to `http://openhabianpi:8080` or the Pi's IP address to access the OpenHAB dashboard.
- **Create an Account**: Follow the on-screen instructions to set up your OpenHAB account, configure devices, and set up your network.

Step 3: Add Devices and Automate

- **Integrate Devices**: Add supported devices using the OpenHAB interface. Devices are categorized based on type (lights, sensors, cameras, etc.) and protocols (Z-Wave, Zigbee, MQTT).
- **Create Automation Rules**: Use OpenHAB's rules engine to set up automation routines for controlling devices based on conditions and triggers, such as turning off lights when everyone leaves the house or adjusting the thermostat based on time.

Benefits of Using an All-in-One Smart Home Platform

Using an all-in-one smart home platform like **Home Assistant** or **OpenHAB** offers several key benefits, making it easier to manage and integrate your smart home devices.

1. Centralized Control

With a smart home hub, you can control all your devices from a single interface. Whether you want to adjust the thermostat, turn on lights, lock the doors, or check security cameras, everything can be done from one app or dashboard.

2. Cross-Device Compatibility

Smart home hubs support a wide range of devices and communication protocols, allowing devices from different manufacturers to work together seamlessly. For example, you can use a **Z-Wave** light switch with a **Zigbee** thermostat and still control them all through the same hub.

3. Customizable Automation

Using a smart home hub allows you to create customized automation rules that fit your lifestyle. You can automate tasks based on triggers such as time, occupancy, weather conditions, or sensor data. For instance, you can automate lights to turn on at sunset or set the thermostat to adjust when you leave for work.

4. Security and Privacy

With a local-only smart home hub, you can maintain greater control over your data, reducing reliance on cloud services and improving privacy. Both **Home Assistant** and **OpenHAB** run locally, meaning your data doesn't need to be sent to external servers, providing you with more security.

5. Scalability

As your smart home grows, adding new devices is easier with a smart home hub. Whether you're adding new sensors, cameras, or even smart appliances, the hub can integrate and manage them all. This scalability ensures that you can continue to expand your smart home without worrying about compatibility.

6. Cost-Effectiveness

By using a Raspberry Pi to run platforms like **Home Assistant** or **OpenHAB**, you can save money on dedicated smart home hubs that might be more expensive. Raspberry

Pi is an affordable, versatile platform that allows you to create a fully functional smart home hub on a budget.

Conclusion

Smart home hubs and platforms like **Home Assistant** and **OpenHAB** provide a powerful and flexible solution for managing your smart home. By setting up these hubs on a **Raspberry Pi**, you can centralize control, automate tasks, and integrate a wide variety of IoT devices, all while ensuring privacy and scalability. Whether you're looking for open-source, customizable solutions or simply want a reliable way to manage your devices, using an all-in-one smart home platform brings efficiency, security, and convenience to your home automation system.

CHAPTER 26

SCALING YOUR SMART HOME SYSTEM

As your smart home setup grows, you'll want to scale your system to manage more devices, expand automation, and ensure smooth operation across multiple areas of your home. Scaling your system involves integrating additional devices, managing multiple hubs or **Raspberry Pi** devices, and incorporating third-party devices into your ecosystem. In this chapter, we'll discuss how to expand your smart home from a small setup to a large one, manage multiple **Raspberry Pi** devices and sensors, and integrate third-party devices into your system seamlessly.

How to Expand and Scale Your Smart Home from a Small Setup to a Large One

Scaling your smart home system is a gradual process that involves upgrading your existing setup, expanding your network, and integrating new devices. When expanding from a small to a larger smart home, it's essential to focus on both performance and reliability to ensure that everything continues to work efficiently.

1. Start with a Solid Foundation

Before scaling, make sure you have a stable and reliable foundation:

- **Choose a Robust Smart Home Platform**: Platforms like **Home Assistant** or **OpenHAB** are perfect for scaling because they are flexible and support numerous devices and integrations.
- **Reliable Network**: Ensure you have a strong network with good coverage. You may need to upgrade your Wi-Fi router, add a **Wi-Fi extender**, or use **mesh networks** to ensure that all devices, especially those spread across larger areas, stay connected.

2. Adding More Devices and Sensors

As your smart home grows, adding more sensors and devices becomes a priority. Begin by adding devices based on specific needs or automation goals, such as expanding security coverage, adding environmental sensors (temperature, humidity, air quality), or upgrading your lighting system.

Tips for Expanding:

- **Device Grouping**: Organize devices into groups by function (e.g., lighting, security, heating) to simplify management and automation.
- **Segmenting Areas**: Scale the system by dividing your home into different areas or zones (e.g., living room, kitchen, garden) and assigning devices to those zones.
- **Z-Wave or Zigbee**: Use mesh-networking protocols like **Z-Wave** or **Zigbee** to connect devices across a large area. These protocols extend the range of devices by using repeaters, which relay data between devices and the hub.

3. Scaling Automation and Rules

With more devices, you'll want to expand your automation to fit a larger system:

- **Complex Automations**: Create more advanced automations that include multiple devices and sensors, such as "Turn on the lights and adjust the thermostat when motion is detected in the living room."
- **Scripting**: Platforms like **Home Assistant** offer scripting capabilities, enabling more granular control of your devices. For example, you could script routines based on occupancy, time of day, or sensor data.

261

4. Network Infrastructure Considerations

As you add more devices, it's crucial to ensure that your network infrastructure can handle the increased load. Consider the following:

- **Mesh Wi-Fi Network**: A **mesh Wi-Fi system** can help extend coverage, particularly in larger homes or areas with spotty Wi-Fi coverage. Mesh systems improve the stability of your network by using multiple access points.
- **Ethernet for Critical Devices**: For devices that require constant connection (e.g., Raspberry Pi hubs, cameras), use Ethernet for a more reliable and faster connection.

Managing Multiple Raspberry Pi Devices and Sensors

When scaling up your smart home, you might use multiple **Raspberry Pi** devices to manage different parts of your home or control various functions. These can act as hubs for different zones or specific devices, or as dedicated controllers for specialized automation tasks.

1. Distributing Raspberry Pi Devices Across Different Areas

One way to scale is by placing multiple **Raspberry Pi** devices in different areas of your home:

- **Central Hub**: Use one **Raspberry Pi** as the main hub to control your entire smart home system (e.g., running **Home Assistant** or **OpenHAB**).
- **Sub-Hubs**: Use additional Raspberry Pi devices as sub-hubs for specific tasks, such as controlling security cameras, environmental sensors, or automating lighting in a particular room.

Example Setup:

- Place a **Raspberry Pi** in the living room to control lighting, a **Raspberry Pi** in the kitchen to manage smart appliances, and another in the security room to manage cameras and sensors.
- Each device can communicate with the central hub to update data, trigger actions, or report status.

2. Managing Communication Between Raspberry Pi Devices

Once you have multiple Raspberry Pi devices, it's essential to ensure they communicate effectively with each other. This can be done using communication protocols like **MQTT, Z-Wave**, or **Zigbee**.

MQTT for Communication:

- Use **MQTT** (Message Queuing Telemetry Transport) to enable your Raspberry Pi devices to communicate with each other. MQTT works well for low-bandwidth, low-latency communication between devices, allowing them to send data (e.g., sensor readings) and trigger actions (e.g., turning on lights).
- Set up an MQTT broker (which can run on one of your Raspberry Pi devices) to handle messages between devices and ensure reliable communication.

3. Using IoT Sensors with Multiple Raspberry Pi Devices

Each Raspberry Pi can be connected to a range of sensors, such as **motion sensors**, **temperature sensors**, and **door/window sensors**. When scaling your setup, you can distribute these sensors across various areas of the home.

Example Setup:

- **Motion Sensors**: Place motion sensors in hallways, the living room, and near doors. Connect each sensor to a different Raspberry Pi, or combine them with one hub.
- **Temperature Sensors**: Use temperature sensors in each room to adjust the thermostat automatically or activate fans when a room gets too hot.

Integrating Third-Party Devices into Your System

A large smart home setup will often involve devices from various manufacturers, each with its own proprietary system or ecosystem. Integrating third-party devices into your system ensures that all your devices work together seamlessly.

1. Using Standardized Communication Protocols

Many third-party devices support open protocols like **Z-Wave**, **Zigbee**, **MQTT**, and **Wi-Fi**, making integration easier. By using a hub like **Home Assistant** or **OpenHAB**, you can connect these devices into one central system.

Example:

- **Z-Wave and Zigbee**: Use **Z-Wave** or **Zigbee hubs** to connect compatible devices, such as locks, sensors, and light bulbs, to your central Raspberry Pi hub.
- **Wi-Fi Devices**: Many Wi-Fi-based devices (like cameras, smart plugs, or thermostats) can easily be added to your system by using compatible integrations in **Home Assistant** or **OpenHAB**.

2. Integrating Smart Appliances and Voice Assistants

You may want to integrate **smart appliances** (e.g., smart fridges, ovens, washing machines) or voice assistants (e.g., **Amazon Alexa**, **Google Assistant**) into your system to expand control and automation.

Example Integration:

- **Smart Appliances**: Use **IFTTT** (If This, Then That) or **MQTT** to connect appliances that are not natively supported by your main platform. For instance, a smart fridge might not directly integrate with **Home Assistant**, but using **IFTTT**, you can trigger an action when a certain condition is met (e.g., sending a notification when the fridge door is left open).
- **Voice Assistant Integration**: Link **Amazon Alexa** or **Google Assistant** to your smart home platform so you can control your devices using voice commands. For example, you can say, "Alexa, turn on the living room lights," and the voice assistant will trigger the corresponding device through the hub.

3. Using APIs and Cloud Services

Some third-party devices and services come with their own cloud-based apps, but you can still integrate them into your home automation system through **APIs** or cloud-based services.

Example Setup:

- **APIs for Cloud Devices**: Devices like **Ring Doorbell, Nest Thermostat,** or **Sonos Speakers** offer APIs that allow integration into your smart home system. By setting up these APIs, you can control these devices from within **Home Assistant** or **OpenHAB**, triggering actions like playing music or adjusting the temperature.
- **Cloud Integrations**: Use services like **IFTTT** to create custom actions between devices, such as sending a notification when a doorbell rings or automatically turning off lights when you leave the house.

Conclusion

Scaling your smart home system from a small setup to a large one involves careful planning, expanding your device network, and integrating new components. By distributing Raspberry Pi devices across different rooms or zones, using reliable communication protocols like **MQTT** and **Z-Wave**, and adding third-party devices through open integrations, you can create a fully expanded smart home that meets your needs. Whether you're adding new sensors, integrating smart appliances, or connecting voice assistants, scaling ensures that your system remains flexible, powerful, and easy to manage.

www.ingramcontent.com/pod-product-compliance
Lightning Source LLC
Chambersburg PA
CBHW070939050326
40689CB00014B/3270